Later Essays

Yone Noguchi

Edited by Edward Marx

2013

Noguchi, Yone, 1875-1947.
Later Essays.
Edited by Edward Marx.
First Edition.

ISBN: 978-0615765433 (paper)

10 9 8 7 6 5 4 3

Later Essays

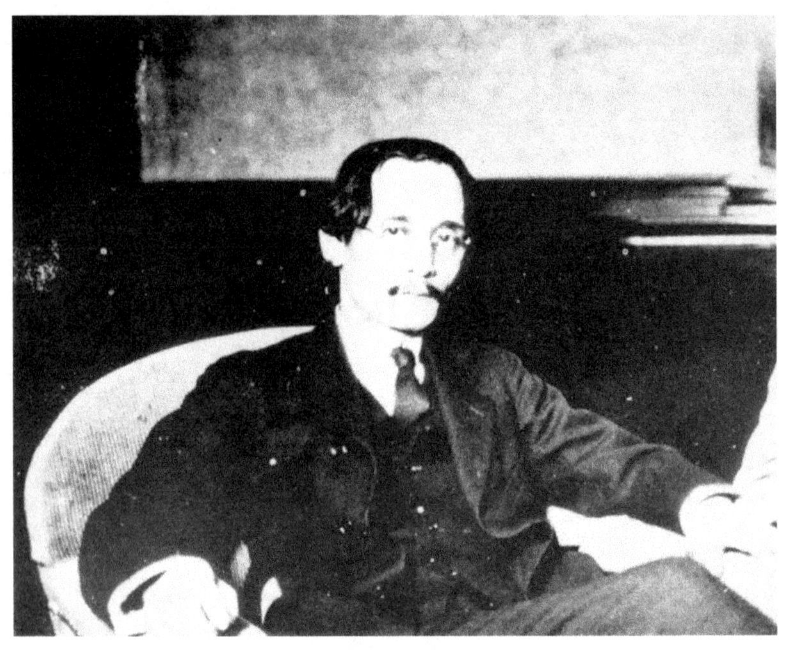

Yone Noguchi in 1926.

Contents

Introduction

Among the Yone Noguchi Papers at the Bancroft Library at the University of California, Berkeley is a set of manuscripts for a book of poems and essays, never published, entitled *The Blood of Silence and Other Poems.* Sent to Isamu Noguchi in March 1948 by his younger half-brother, Tomiji Noguchi, it is made up of remnants of material their late father had been trying to publish since the 1920s. Tomiji hoped, he wrote in a prefatory note, that the book would be "both epilogue and prelude for the international poetical works of Yone Noguchi after a long interval of this war." There was, he thought, "a sort of Providence for the curious fate, not being buried in oblivion." By this point, however, there was too much oblivion and not enough providence: the odd assortment that had somehow escaped the bombing of Noguchi's Tokyo house in April 1945 was in no condition to be published. Even if Isamu had been inclined to take up the heavy task of reviving the reputation of the father he still resented, he would have found few publishers still interested in the man who "discarded his Western wife and ideas" and "became a great booster of Japanese imperialism," according to his *Time* obituary.[1]

In the more optimistic days of the 1920s and 1930s, Noguchi had envisioned separate volumes of poems and essays. His Keio University colleague Sherard Vines wrote in 1925 of "a considerable body of poems . . . which will shortly appear in book form under the title 'The Blood of Silence,'" that was to be "of the greatest importance to Noguchi students, recording, as it does, a substantial advance."[2] Eight years later Noguchi had enlisted no less an editor than Marianne Moore as his supporter for a collection of essays. "I am hell bent on helping him if I can," Moore told William Rose Benét of the *Saturday Review*. "He wants me to get the Viking Press to sponsor for England and America a set of essays he is having published in Tokyo and I thought it would help if I offered one or two to magazines."[3]

That these essays remained uncollected and for the most part forgotten, despite the enthusiasm of Marianne Moore and others, makes this volume of *Later Essays* an appropriate title to inaugurate this new series of Noguchi Project editions. The essays are, indeed, an epilogue and a prologue, helping to complete our understanding of Noguchi's later development and thought, and preparing the ground for a new assessment of his contribution to English literature, in which he served as Japan's most prominent representative for four decades, a crucial link between Eastern and Western modernists who contributed substantially to the internationalization of Japanese poetry, drama and art.

Noguchi's work always provoked highly divergent responses, and his essays were no exception. "I do not know whether the essay is a Japanese literary form but if it is not," an English critic, Francis Bickley, once wrote, "Mr. Noguchi has perfectly realised its possibilities, and has used it in a manner which makes our most delicate masters seem rather heavy-handed."[4] Yet Arthur Waley, writing of the same volume of essays, *Through the Torii*, criticized Noguchi's "desire to gallop before he can trot, to be decorative and epigrammatic before he is even securely intelligible."[5] The twenty-two essays collected here represent, for the most part, an advance on his earlier work and are essential reading for any student of Noguchi's work. They are not without faults: stylistic and grammatical quirks, obscure references, shoddy scholarship, self-promotion, and overbearing nationalism come readily to mind. Noguchi no doubt would have cheerfully acknowledged them. "Full of faults, you say. / What beauty in repentance! / Tears, songs . . . thus life flows," he had once written. He explains in one of the essays: "the language I use is not that of people born to it; it is the English I picked up at will and arranged as I pleased." Out of his "renovated language of unimpaired connotation," as Marianne Moore called it, Noguchi created one of the distinctive international voices in twentieth-century English prose. "The delightful thing about the essays," wrote another admirer, Padraic Colum, "is that they really are essays—not editorials, not manifestos, not compressed systems; each is according to Dr. Johnson's definition—'a loose sally of the mind,' vagrant, unpretentious, spontaneous . . . we rediscover, as we read what is here expressed with a real and an unconscious humility, a world that has life and beauty and simplicity."[6]

The periodicals that opened their columns for these essays included *The Dial* before its demise, John Middleton Murry's *Adelphi*, and a handful of other periodicals in Britain and the United States. Noguchi was not aggressive in his publication efforts; if Marianne Moore could not accept his "Harunobu" essay for *The Dial*, he told her in 1929, "send it back to me, because there is no other magazine fit for this article in America."[7] In the mid-1930s he briefly found a receptive market in international English-language magazines in India and China. With his lecture tour of India in 1934-5, the *Calcutta Review* published his three lectures on Japanese art, poetry, and No drama, while his visits to Shanghai led to an invitation to contribute to Shanghai's progressive new international magazine, the *T'ien Hsia Monthly*.[8] These essays, for the most part translations of his larger body of Japanese prose writing, offer a substantial sample of his later thought and style.

Noguchi closed his last English essay, a brief essay on "The Future of Democracy" written specially for the *New Republic* in May 1937, with the optimistic words: "Look forward with hope, believe in the future." But full-scale war between Japan and China broke out two months later, bringing to a grinding halt the revival of his career as an international essayist.

The essays in this volume were published between 1928 to

1937 and represent all of Noguchi's known English essays from 1922 until the end of his life, excepting variant versions and Noguchi's essays on Japanese artists.[9]

EDWARD MARX

Random Thoughts on Japanese Poetry

I often think that impersonality is but a psychological state of mind which knows nothing of strait-laced intellect, the purity of which keeps itself quite apart from a personality often vulgar. The highest endeavour of poets, at least in old Japan, I think, was to create a poetical personality out of the primitive strength of that impersonality. Therefore poetry in Japan, when it is good, is nothing but the nuance of impersonality, that strangely turns to personality which we sometimes understand as individuality. Such poetry, natural but paradoxical enough, is far more personal than what is generally called personal.

Now see the Uta-poems of Saigyo or the Hokku-poems of Basho. Perhaps you will find in them the living proof of what I mean. These poets hold the mystery of a rope-dancer walking between the two extremities, the personal and impersonal; this mystery, as I once wrote, hanging in the air of perfume as a web, and swaying in music soft and vivid, leads me to exclaim: "Oh, what a creation of surprise dancing on the wire of golden impulse! What an elf of light and shadow, what a flash of beauty, again, what a moth-light playing on reality's dusk!"

It is one of my joys to read these little poems in the grey soft atmosphere in my study on the outskirts of Tokyo, when an autumn rain falls with song of suggestion on the quest of poetry. It is my belief to say that any poetry, when it is true, should not be troubled with an intellect which wants to discover meaning before beauty in the work.

Attitude of Western Poets

I know of course that the attitude of western poets in discovering the meaning of life or recreating it is admirable; and I do understand well enough why they ascribe importance to an intellectual power. But a great literary danger, I dare say, lies in it, because there is nothing more sad for poets than to enslave themselves to intellect. Indeed they are miserable when they know no other way of expressing their own poetry than relying on intellect. And when that intellect exaggerates its own authority, I think I know nothing more miserable than that. The intellect in such a case often proves itself to be a savage hero, who makes beauty fly away as a fool acts toward an angel. It is a narrow-minded egoist whose dogma is always blind to an artistic harmony, but glad to play at vandalism openly. I am happy to think that our Japanese poems, when they are good, are but a thing that denies the encroachment of intellect. Even from this point alone, they are something worthy to take notice of.

Once I wrote as follows: "It is said in the west that the poets are a race apart. The fact that our Japanese poets are not a race apart, should be the very focus for a discussion of Japanese poets. While in the west the poets claim special regard and, indeed, immortality for themselves, we in Japan treat the poet as a natural phenomenon, as natural as a flower or bird. I admit that we Japanese as poets are lacking in creative power, and do not aim, like many western poets, at becoming rebuilders of life.

"We are taught not to deal with poetry as a mere art, but to look upon it as the most necessary principle along which our real life shall be developed. When we kneel before poetry, it is our desire to create a clarified pure realm where we can, through the inspiration of rhythm, arrange our own minds. And we recognize the existence of the compromising ground of passion, where we as members of society found our safety. What great uncompromising creators of passion were Shelley, Byron, Browning, and Swinburne! They were so earnest in their desire for the recreation of life, and not afraid were they, when their desire reached its climax, even to risk, reaching a condition of confused intricacy. They were indeed great and wonderful heroes. We cannot help thinking, on the other hand, what cowards the majority of Japanese poets have been."

Admitting our cowardice as poets, we want to create an atmosphere which is impersonal, not touched or wounded by the sharpness of vulgar individualism; even as a reader of our Japanese poems, we must have that atmosphere soft and grey, and read them with appreciation or love but not with criticism, because it is our own part to make them perfect and whole, since they are imperfect and half-made in themselves. Therefore the function of the readers in Japan is as important as that of the poets. And that function should be accomplished with appreciation but not with criticism. Criticism is an art more or less cynical, that a man tired or ill in health is apt to play with. But one who has the fullness of love which disarms criticism, and moves beautifully life's orchestra of the five senses, can fully command the art of appreciation.

Real Joy And Sorrow

When we read appreciatively the old poetical work called "Man-yo Shu" or the Hokku poems of Basho or Buson, I am sure that appreciation makes them soon a real part of ourselves, therefore our own vital question of body and soul; and thus we will never be able to think of them separately from our personal love. I am happy to say that we find our own lives in these works, in which all Japanese love or longing toward nature and life, in one word, all dreams of heaven and earth now appear and then disappear like a shadow written or erased by clouds. There is a real Japanese joy and sorrow in them, for which we are thankful to be led away into a world of spiritual beauty.

These old poetical works of Japan are wonderful indeed in making the natural phenomenon express a rare moment when emotion awakes and still more wonderful in making them suggest the rarest moment when that emotion suddenly subsides. The feminine susceptibility of a Japanese poet commands more delicately its own situation, when his technical skill, often imperfect, melts his own self into the subjects he treats. It is said that the man of genius is feminine; so are most of our Japanese poets. As a poet of feminine personality, at least when he writes, it is natural that the moon, flowers and birds are the subjects of his passionate selection. He sings of them as a soloist, not as the author of orchestra. He is a lyrist. When I read these lyrics which treat of one mood or thought, whatever it might be, I find them to be various in their own expression; but they are strangely generalised with the key-note of simplicity. This simplicity is the only citadel where the Japanese poetry rises or falls.

When Simplicity Is Misused

There is nothing more sad for art, I know, than the time when simplicity is misused, in which from the failure of simplicity emphasis degenerates into exaggeration. Of course we have enough examples to prove this sad poetical affair. And it is true also that the rhythm of poetry with a simple key-note like that of our Japanese poems, is always changeless, and gives one such a feeling of lassitude that will end as something like an unbearable grief. It is no use to say that our poems, when they are good, are a thing most perfect and audacious, a thing already reached the climax, for which none other course opens but to perish with its own creator. When we see that no real second Hitomaro and Basho appeared in the Japanese poetical annals, it is easy to understand that their art was so perfect that no follower of their schools was able to take a step forward in his artistic exploitation.

Talking on Japanese poetry, I often dwelt on morality in connection with it, and on this matter I once wrote in the following fashion:

"We Japanese have also our own literary danger. I mean,

that we often mistake a simple and cold morality for an art. I should like to know what is a more dangerous thing for poets than this sad morality. There are only a few Japanese poets who have failed from their abuse of moods and passions; but we know so many cases wherein their poetical failure was quite complete under the stifling breath of conventional morality. This damage would not necessarily be below that inflicted by intellect; it might be greater.

"We notice that the western poets often attempt to discover a poetical theory even in the waving plaits of Apollo's robe, and analyze intellectually a little cloud flying in the sky. Admitting that their poetical theory and intellectual are doubtless great, I have no hesitation in that it is they who harden, shrink, and wither their own art. It is true to say that they owe much to the matter of form for the great development of their epics and dramas. Also it is true that the undeveloped form of Japanese poetry has given a mighty freedom for our poets to fly into an invisible spiritual domain. We can say again that, if these poets both of the west and the east often stray into the field of non-poetry, it is the result of their too close attachment to form."

When I compare Japanese poems with the dew upon lotus leaves of green or under maple leaves of red, shining, glittering and sparkling, now pearl-white, then amethyst-blue, again ruby-red, or with a spider-thread laden with the white summer dews, swaying among the branches of a tree like an often invisible ghost in air, I mean that their authors beautifully transcended the form which is slight in reality, and flew into the spiritual kingdom. In the hands of such a great poet the form of thirty-one syllables or seventeen syllables would appear surely as if a seven-coloured rainbow. Certainly the Japanese poems are delicate. And also the minds of Japanese readers should be equally delicate, when they are to appreciate them fully. I cannot forget one American lady who came to see me one morning at the poppy-covered mountain-side of California where I used to live some 30 years ago. What I cannot forget chiefly about that morning was her story that she made a round-about way in entering into my garden, as the proper path had been blocked by a spider-net thick with diamond-dews. I exclaimed then as I do often even today: "Such a sweet soul that could not dare break that silvery thread of one spider, would be the very soul to appreciate our Japanese poetry." And how glad I was to know that even in America there was such a woman who was so responsive to such a trifling beauty of natural existence.

For One Really Appreciative

To a casual reader our Japanese poems may not mean anything, but to a person who is really appreciative, they would appear as a search-light or flash of passion or thought cast on a moment of life and nature, which, by virtue of its intensity, leads one to the conception of the whole. The Japanese poems are a piece often isolated, swift and discontinuous; but it is the appreciation of readers, as I said before, to make them complete and whole. There the real value of them may be only measured by what mood or illusion they inspire in the reader's mind. Even if we cannot become a poet, we must try to become a real reader.

Let me tell you one story, a true experience I had now almost 30 years ago, which made me awake to the beauty of nature. That is the story of my call on Yeiki Kikakudo, the descendant of the famous Hokku poet Kikaku in poetical lineage, who used to live in his seventieth year at a little cottage on a hill in Shiba Park, Tokyo. I cannot recollect now exactly how I happened to call on him one night, except from my impulse or feeling that my meeting with him was necessary for my poetical development. It was the night of Meigetsu, the full moon of September when many wanderers like myself, a human moth restless after soul's sensation, could be seen in the park through the shadows of trees.

The Moonlight

The little house, I mean that of Master Yeiki, so small that it might be comfortably put in any ordinary-sized Western drawing-room, was deadly silent with no light lighted; I thought at once that it was the poet's beautiful consideration towards the moon whose heavenly light, not being disturbed by any earthly lamp, might thus have full sway of splendor. I met the old poet when I called, sitting on the door step under the golden shower of the moon-light, when I climbed up to his little house. He led me into the house where the all open shoji doors welcomed the moon with old-fashioned hospitality. I thought then that it should be the way to treat the celestial guest; when I observed how the Japanese moonlight crawled in with its fairy-like golden steps I simply wondered how it was humanized here. We two, young and old, sat silent, leaving all the talk to the breeze which carried down the moon's autumnal message; the light fell on the hanging scroll at the Tokonoma, whereon I read the following Hokku poem:

> Autumn's full moon:
> Lo, the shadows of a pine tree
> Upon the mats!

Really it was my first opportunity to observe the full beauty of the light and shadow, more the beauty of the shadow in fact far more luminous than the light itself with such a decorativeness, particularly when it stamped the dustless mats as a strange-shaped ageless pine tree. I thanked Kikaku, the author of the above lines, for giving me just the point where to find the natural beauty. I bowed to the Poet Yeiki in place of saying good-night, and thanked him for the most interesting talk, although we had spoken scarcely a word, but I was in a delightful mood as already then the old story of Carlyle and Emerson who had a happy chat in silence was known to me. When I left Yeiki's house, the moon was quite high in the sky, and all the trees and birds were blessed by the golden light of it. And it was exactly such a moon-night on which many years later I wrote the following lines:

Across the song of night and moon,
(Oh perfume of perfumes!)
My soul, as a wind
Whose heart's too full to sing,
Only roams astray.

And again it was such a moon-night when the greatest Hokku poet, Basho Matsuo, wrote the following impromptu:

Shall I knock
At Miidera Temple's gate?
Ah, moon of to-night!

Suppose you stand at Miidera Temple's gate high upon the hill lapped and again lapped by the slow water, with your face toward Lake Biwa which, as a certain poetess has written, "like a shell of white lies dropped by the passing day," I am sure you will feel yourself to be a god or goddess, who by accident or mystery has risen above the silvery mists which softly covered the earth of later night I do not mean to imply that the Japanese poems, whether they be Hokku or Uta, are lyrical poetry in the general western understanding; but the Japanese mind gets the effect before perceiving the fact of their brevity, their sensibility resounding to their single note, as the calm bosom of river water to the song of a bird.

Magic of Japanese Poems

One of the English critics exclaimed from his enthusiasm over Japanese poetry: "That is valuable as a talisman rather than as a picture. It is a pearl to be dissolved in the wine of a mood. Pearls are not wine, nor in themselves to be thought of as a drink, but there is a kind of magic in the wine in which they are dissolved." That magic of Japanese poems is the real essence of lyrical poetry even of the highest order. I do not see why we cannot call them musical, when we call the single note of a bird musical; indeed they attain to a condition, as Pater once remarked, which music alone completely realizes, because what they aim at and practice is the evocation of mood or psychological intensity, not the physical explanation.

As once I wrote, today we must readjust the meanings of all things or give a new interpretation to all the old meanings; and we must solve the problem of life and the world, from our real obedience to laws and knowledge that will make the inevitable tum to a living song, and learn the true meaning of time from the evanescence of psychical life. Then our human life will become true and living. I do not mean that the Japanese poems alone would help us in making our lives worthy to live; but I believe that they are one of the things without which our human lives would appear empty. I take this opportunity to thank again for the service of the Japanese poems showered on us in the past; and I believe that it will last for many years to come.

Japan Today and Tomorrow (Osaka), December 1928

Psychology of Modern Japan

A Nation of Compromisers Which Has Lost Its Standards

Believe me that I am not one who takes a pleasure in looking over the matter with cold blood or sarcasm. But when I think about how the psychology of the present Japanese mind is working, I cannot help pointing out, first of all the shortness of spiritual vitality; talking about it with my friend, I said to him often with passion: "Look at the faces of the present Japanese, only eager to conciliate and compromise, glad to make concessions! Is it unfair to say that they are the faces of street-stallmen on a fête day at worst, and of secretaries or clerks at best? Is it untrue to say that they only know how to appreciate material things?" People who lay stress on materialism, I should say, belong to a third-rate nation; although I do not know where to find first-class people who look far ahead, searching into the truth beyond materialism to the point in which it yields to reality, I know that the Japanese of present day, using the words of Tennyson's "Morte D'Arthur," "either from lust of gold, or like a girl valuing the giddy pleasure of the eyes," have lost power to focus their glasses on an object, spiritual as well as material. Shortly, they have become people who cannot resolve the superficial compound into its elements. Their minds are rattling, their souls are lukewarm.

Avoid Compromise

For the past twenty years I have been lecturing to my home people on the importance of real life, absolute but not compromising, created out of freedom; I did not know how otherwise we could make a first-class country out of Japan. But when I seek in vain today for a face with wild and glad eyes, with an expression of anger or prayer, such a face as Carlyle's, a face at which stones or shouts of Banzai are sometimes thrown, I cannot help calling Japan a country of street-stallmen or secretaries. In the past, at least at the Restoration days or the beginning time of New Japan, there were Japanese, prophetic because they lighted the darkness with their own lamps of truth, however small these lamps might have been, they were real because they saved the others at the same time as they saved themselves. How often I advised the Japanese of present day not to be afraid of standing in the painful forefront of reality, and to set hope on the future, not merely on the present. How often I said that while being ignorant and narrow-minded in the modern sense, the Japanese of the past walked on life's highway, simple and straight, that led them into idealism. When they did not know how to compromise with the others, their homogeneity was a dominant force that adjusted their own kingdom.

Old Traditions Lost

But how have the present Japanese become people of compromise, superficially clever and inwardly weak-minded? When the so-called modern education deprived Japan of her old tradition, it should take a great part of responsibility for the spiritual languidness from which we are suffering. Although I am not a curser of modern civilization, I often think that when it was imported into Japan as an "imitative education," it caused us to lose our sense of vision, because the Western civilization dazzled and charmed us, first of all, with its catalogues and theories, and then made us miserable talking machines, led by other people. There is nothing more sad than to become a tributary province; and that is the spiritual condition of present Japan.

Quite natural for the talking machine, we present Japanese

take a pleasure in speech, in spite of tragedy in which the dignity of speech is lost. Talking on Carlyle who managed to escape from madness through his gift of speech, I always say that the respect of silence makes speech more effective; if there is no austerity of silence behind it, that becomes action in actual life, speech would be a ripple of life's water, a mere touching of the surface of things or life. Speech is today a sort of banjo or guitar which a secretary or clerk, not qualified with the seriousness of a madman, plays for amusement. When I insist on the returning of speech to its original power, I am emphasizing the importance of spiritual honesty, since it is a fountain-head which freedom, introspection and many of the best human qualities spring forth like soul-gladdening water out of a valley. Japan of the present day, I regret to say, lacks spiritual honesty.

Copying the West's Worst

I cannot blame Japan, when I consider the circumstances under which she is situated, that she models herself on the likeness of Western countries, and the Japanese, one and all, from a cabinet minister down to shopkeepers or street pedlars, are far more interested in their worst aspects than their best, because the vulgarity of the former is more attractive than the virtue of the latter. The trouble is, I always say, that our country began the new regime by copying only the last chapter of the record of Western civilization, and had no time to investigate how such a result had been reached there. Besides, the geographical situation should be taken into account, because Japan, being situated at the furthest eastern end of the world, is something like a pool or puddle, safely apart from the rushing current of a main stream, into which all sorts of Western phenomena, spiritual as well as material, find their own way, and expect to stay till they die their own natural death. In truth there is no country in the world like this country where the adjustment is impossible, and discrimination has neither rule nor measure; from another point of view in which Japan, as a subject state of the west, has to buy anything or everything that the west commands, she is another instance which proves that poor countries live more expensively than wealthy.

Back to Paganism

I always think that under such a condition it is foolish to talk here about democracy of Western origin, because it is sometimes interpreted as a kind of socialism from which idealism has been out, or even as a sort of communism without a theory that asserts itself. Not only in the question of democracy but all the other matters, spiritual or material, our interpretations are frighteningly various only to suit ro our sentimentalism or whim; in the long history of Japan, there is no time as today when such confusing weakness distracts Japanese minds. If there is the thing that might save us from mental ruin, it would be paganism; the propagation of paganism might reduce all heterogeneous absurdities into element, and pull back my country into its own original senses.

If I am mistaken for a conservative, I say nothing against it, because my conservatism is only progressionism that becomes serious; and if I am criticised, patriotism only begins when the naked truth is plainly told.

The Trans-Pacific, 26 January 1929

Insect Musicians and Others

I am besieged just now by a musical regiment of autumn insects, at my home not far from Tokyo. The crickets, bell-insects—that is to say, *calytoryphus marmoratus, homaeogryllus japonicus*—and others strike their instruments in all sorts of tune, high and low, sharp and flat. At my home, I think I may be the only listener to this nocturnal orchestra that nature plays, and I cannot help thanking God for this great privilege of living close to the ground. Two sides of my house open to a patch of land overgrown with weeds; perhaps this is the reason I enjoy a better orchestra of insect-musicians here than at the homes of my friends.

"Now I turn over. O crickets, step aside if you please!" Such is Issa's *hokku* poem, if I remember rightly, written one October night at his mountain home in Shinshu when he was besieged by autumn insects. Should I be aware at my home of a cricket singing behind a picture at the alcove, or by the transom window of a bedroom, this Lilliputian poem of Issa comes to my mind. Basho wrote a *hokku* verse at Genju-An, a hillside cottage near Ishiyama, meaning: "I have no treat to offer you except the fact that mosquitoes are small here." (*Waga yado wa ka no chiisaki wo chiso kana.*) Then I should be glad to assume a poetical attitude as if to say: "Come to my home and listen to the music that insects play—that is my offering." In the past a Japanese poet, great or small, wrote about autumn insects and their music. There is no better season, in truth, to those of us who are in accord with nature, than the time in October when putting away all lights, we listen to the nocturnal orchestra of insects.

I wish now to speak of flowering plants. Except a large tree like crêpe myrtle of which I once wrote:

> Its trunk and branches, while looking like a leper's
> fingers or arms holding Koyasan's slope,
> Tremble with joy in its red soul drawn toward the
> sun,

nearly all the flowering plants in autumn bloom close to the ground. I am not discussing here whether morning-glory belongs to summer or autumn; but it seems that a better species of it begins from late August to early September. Whenever I speak of flowering plants in the fall, I must first point out a hagi-flower—to use the botanical name, *lespedeza*—the graceful form of which is so sinuous as not to spill dew-drops in the morning. I know that western people would take the majority of so-called "flowering seven grasses" only for weeds. Remembering how our Japanese poets in the past discovered their beauty, I cannot but be thankful for that poetical service. Otherwise we might say, like a foreigner, that these "seven grasses" in autumn are but weeds in Sunday clothes. What is the real work of the poet? My answer is short: "Discovering new beauty in nature." How sharp and discriminating is the eyesight of our poets! They are not scientific chroniclers of a theory lying between the stars. They are modest, noticing but the little part of nature by their feet; small enough, but large enough when it tells them how to understand nature, and how to praise its beauty. As quantity, the world of their discovery would be insignificant; but who can doubt its spiritual value? Their discovery may be no more than a nameless flowering plant or fallen petal or trivial bird; we cannot ignore it, however, since there is in it a suggestion of the great universe. Their singing may be fragmentary and broken; the poets I revere could not compete with others in the matter of quantity. There is psychological value in the quality of things.

I thank Japanese poets of the past for giving me this little natural world, from which I am able to step into a larger world. The real poetry, whatever it be, is but a little gate of mystery through which we go into a world of Eternity complete and round. Once I wrote: "Between petals of flower there is a little invisible gate. We poets are a Tobinori-taro, accommodating himself to all circumstances, or a long-nosed goblin, a will-o'-the-wisp, in sudden appearance and disappearance." Our Japanese poets, when they are best, are that long-nosed goblin or Tobinori-taro. I wrote also: "In poetry the revival of nature or, to use another word, reality, is not our purpose. When our power of adjustment with nature is perfect, our objectivity becomes settled, and our poetry free from photographic realism, a thing that is vulgar." Entering the season of autumn, we find our objectivity losing its curiosity; and our poetry steadily rising to the high mark of its own spiritual worth. After all one is not an objective creature, but a subjective being.

Japanese poets in the past, it seems, could not think of autumn without a sense of sorrow. The greatest interpreter of autumn as a symbol of sorrow, was, as we know, the priest Saigyo who made it seem natural for us to look upon autumn with sorrow's tear. It is said that when Dante Gabriel Rossetti had painted a sickly-looking lady with long yellow hair, all the ladies of the time were, in look, affected by his lady in the picture. I myself have written many autumn poems from the angle of sorrow; but if autumn is the symbol of sorrow, that sorrow should be one which makes autumn still more beautiful and noble.

We must adjust and put in order what our ancestors thought and dreamed. Keats sings of grapes, apples, gourds, and hazelnuts, and of autumn as the season of fruition; we Japanese too have the phrase: "In autumn the sky is high and the horses become fat." There is nothing more delightful to see than nature's fruition; when nature becomes mellow and mature, her beauty is so decorative. If you doubt me, you have only to observe how chestnuts, meaty and reddish-brown, burst from the prickly burs. Look at a persimmon tree covered with golden balls and see how a Siberian kite flies in the high sky, pretending to be an aeroplane.

I would praise autumn as the season of decorative beauty in nature; and again, as the season of fruition. In an essay entitled The Art of the Little World, I wrote: "Nature is made in accordance with a decorative plan, and is coloured accordingly. We have the special privilege of differentiating her beauty. When a Western critic speaks of Japanese art, he includes it in one word, decorative. I am not saying that he is wrong; but he is lacking, apparently, in discrimination. Not only in art but humanly this decorative beauty should be an evidence of personality, for we human beings are to be taken also as an art. We must do our best to appear decoratively." I know that I am in accord with nature, when I lose myself in her decorative beauty.

Dealing with autumn, artists like Korin or Hoitsu were always decorative; their work was not disfigured by so much as a touch of sentimental sorrow. They were, in this respect at least, international. My autumnal emotion often begins pessimistically; but I forget sadness as soon as I enter the psychological kingdom of subjectivity.

The Dial, July 1929

My Ideal Home

When I try to choose a spot for my ideal home, not far from Heaven and yet not far from town, Ichijoji Village, south and west of the Hiyei Mountain, comes to my mind, because Basho of the seventeenth century found there a temporary nest. Buson, poet and artist of a century later, when he canvassed for the rebuilding of Basho's old home in the village back on the hill by the Konpukuji Temple, dwelt reminiscently upon the place with its solitary old mosses and dozing birds among the trees, though sufficiently humanized by a grog-shop and a bean-curd seller. I love this Ichijoji Village not only because of Basho's association with it, but also because of Jozan Ishikawa, who, jealously guarding the solitude of forty years' self-confinement, built here Shisendo, the "Hall of the Poets," where he read the classics and studied calligraphy. Of course, there is no reason why I should follow these Oriental Timons in choosing an ideal spot, since any old place at the frontier of Heaven and the world suits me well enough, provided that in summer the cicadas sing. I want to see how my loneliness will grow when besieged and attacked by their burning song, a prayer or a curse. I am a summer poet, if I am anything at all.

If I were a Jozan, I am not sure that I would object to crossing the Kamo river, saying, as Jozan once replied to the Emperor of his time who invited him, "Though the water be shallow, ashamed I will be to have my old wrinkles reflected there." Nor have I any desire to be called, as he was, Kisei-no-koshi, the "man of supreme calibre." Moreover, I admit the life of solitude only as far as a modern sense of living would allow. At Shisendo there is a large wooden tablet hung on the wall, one of the few relics in Jozan's own hand, in which the Chinese character of Hsien, meaning leisure, is written in the fashion of the Chin dynasty when T'ao Ch'ien forgot the appointment of Fate while gazing at the southern hill. I wonder if the very soul of a man of high character does not exhaust itself in that one word—leisure. He whose hours exist only on the face of a clock is a worldling, a philistine, an earthworm. What a joy it is to feast on leisure in an ideal home, and like Whitman, to "loaf and invite one's soul, observing a spear of summer grass!" Although to Whitman the grass was entrancing as God's handkerchief or a hieroglyphic common to Tackahoe and Congressman, we Japanese do not feel at home without a pine tree in the garden, its shadow stealing into the guest-room in the moonlight like a Claude Duval dancing a shadowy coranto.

One who has visited Jozan's Shisendo knows that the view towards Kyoto in the distance over the valley is not without delight. Of course, Jozan must have loved it like a scholar of leisure, as it shifted and changed according to the season, since he left us twelve poems in praise of it. But if I say to you that scenery of surpassing beauty should not be seen all the time, for a beautiful woman looks more beautiful if we have only an occasional sight of her, I am afraid that you will call me an uninvited cynic. Perhaps I am. As that cynic, I once insisted that a friend who lived by the beautiful Zushi bay overlooking Kamakura and Yenoshima in the mists, should make a blind which should be raised only occasionally. It is from the same motive that if I lived here at Shisendo as a Jozan of the twentieth century, I would not hesitate to block by a sliding wooden door the western view towards the city of the old capital.

Today, nothing remains to tell us with what books, poems or prose, he filled the space of his mind in grand leisure. In one of my Japanese essays I wrote: "Suppose my study facing the south with a verandah in the shape of an L. I would place a table at the turn of the verandah, on which you would find many works of the Elizabethan dramatists, Webster, Ford and

Dekker. Shakespeare, although, as Emerson said, an omnipresent humanity co-ordinated in all his faculties is altogether too great for my quiet mind to select. The calibre of Marlowe is more to my fancy." Of late I confess that my love of books has greatly ebbed. But if I had a library in my ideal home, I would take out from its shelves Sir Philip Sidney's sonnets or, better than that, Lamb's *Christ's Hospital.* And with the book in my hand, I would lay me down on a bench or hammock in the garden, supposing I have one, where the pine tree hums a hymn. Certainly the wind would blow gently in my garden.

I have read that the ex-emperor Reigen once paid a visit to Jozan at Shisendo, and was received where the autumnal wind was sweetest; with its aerial accompaniment the retired scholar and poet, according to the book, played the *Koto* much to the ex-emperor's delight. It was the very moment for Jozan to exclaim as at a later date Landor exclaimed: "By the blessing of God, I am Walter Savage Landor!" I do not know what I should say were I similarly situated; perhaps as was Jozan before the ex-emperor, I would be silent, bending my humble head down to the ants busy in their traffic among the nameless grasses of the garden.

I love a bamboo thicket and, if I have my own ideal home, I shall place one in the back yard. It is delightful to receive a tropical touch from the bamboo leaves scorching in the summer light. But how lonely it would be to hear the sudden sound of the stalks breaking in a snowy night! I am a Japanese like Saigyo of the twelfth century, a vagabond priest and poet, who exclaimed: "Alas, without loneliness I should be more lonely,— so I keep it!" It was Kyorai, one of Basho's ardent followers, who listened to the nocturnal cry of a cuckoo while the midnight moonlight strayed into the bamboo thicket. There is nothing like the voice of a bird to break the night stillness and make my poetical mood leap.

It is said that Jozan during his life of retirement had no more than seven friends. Seven friends would be a good number for any person. But when he passed away at the grand old age of ninety, some one hundred people from the neighbouring villages, according to an old book, attended his funeral, weeping and longing for his high character. Observing seven moral codes, he led a most frugal life on barley and beans. he hung on the wall of his kitchen a tablet, "Beware of gluttony!" which reminds me of Wordsworth at Dove Cottage charging his guest for an extra boiled egg.

The name the "Hall of the Poets," originated in the fact that, as can still be seen there, Jozan placed in one of the rooms thirty six portraits of distinguished Chinese poets and writers of various dynasties. It amuses me to think that, if he lived today, he would select great names of the west according to his own whim, not merely copying the dome of the British Museum. But I must be content with my present home in spite of the aggression of modern life, believing, as T'ao Ch'ien believed, in the decrees of Fate and content to live out my allotted span. It is only possible to adjust, as best I can, the things before my eyes with hope for tomorrow, and if the house be dusty and full of spider's webs, I will sweep and clean it again with hope for tomorrow. One of Jozan's aphorisms says: "Remember dusters and the broom!" The cleaning of one's house comes properly before the cleaning of the soul. Am I growing to the age of respect for dusting as a creditable work for an old man?

The Spectator, 15 February 1935

With Fuji Mountain It Begins and Ends

My adoration of nature that begins with Fuji Mountain, will end with it. Long is my journey in the world of poetry; I find, now looking backwards, that I have been already travelling there for some forty years. When I think of the mercy of nature, I return at once, neither time nor place being questioned, to a boy who looked up at Fuji Mountain for the first time, and like Basho of the 17th century, whose dream at his death bed "ran about the autumnal moorland," I wander by the plain about the foot of this mountain where the graceful curves of beauty are drawn. Roaming "by the plain" are not the right words, because I looked up to the holy circular cone of Fuji Mountain only to adore it from the distance of the lower plain.

As a wretched-looking country boy I took the first view of Fuji Mountain from the rough sea where our steamer, as ridiculous a little thing as one could imagine, that left Yokkaichi for Tokyo, found itself drifting at the mercy of the waves early in the morning. It was the month of February whose cutting wind blew up the curtain and made my play, "Adoration of Nature," begin. I saw for the first time a grand matchless symbol of God in Fuji Mountain, of which I was afraid in reverence. If I had not been impressed then with a sense of poetry that the mountain suggested, I believe that my life would have never been developed as a poet. My adoration of nature begins and ends with this great mountain, and my poet-life also begins and ends with it. The life of a poet, I think, exhausts itself in these three words, "Adoration of Nature."

My poetical mind is always governed by the psychology of the first impression. Natural phenomena too are revealed by their own special gesticulations, now fearful and now tender, at the moment when one comes first in contact with them. Since I saw first Fuji Mountain in my sixteenth year of age, I do not know how many times I have looked up to its inspiring form from a place far away or near by. Some nine years ago when I left my native shore for America, our steamer that had waved a farewell to the Kannonzaki promontory a few hours before, now became wrapped by an evening shadow that dropped on the ocean, changing gradually from gray to brown. I stood on the deck with my head turning towards the low sky that I had left, and there I found somebody standing all alone, giving me a voiceless send-off. Was it a ghost? No! It was but the circular cone of Fuji Mountain picked out against the sky with dark purple. The circumstances, I confess, gave me a sad lonesome feeling such as I never felt before. Tears choked me. Fuji Mountain at that moment was the ideal perfection of beauty entering the suggestive realm of sorrow, the most august sight in the world. But whenever I shut my eyes to draw a Fuji Mountain in my mind the very Fuji Mountain which I saw when I was sixteen years old, appears and speaks to me in the most familiar language. I spent many years abroad, and on not a few occasions that discouraged and made me sick with despair, the Fuji Mountain of my boyish days stirred my mind and spirit with the following words: "I protect you! Do not fear, but stand up and rise high in the sky! I lead you righteously! The path which you have to follow is straight. Only in the path of justice, a flower of diligence blooms, and divine air courses. Make your life wider and nobler!" Again the same Fuji Mountain would often say that it would become a spiritual ladder to me for climbing up the sky, and would teach me how to open the gate of mystery and creep into the hall of prayer. I am glad that under its blessing I managed to keep my simplicity of mind and thought, and found life's only road, that is, the road of poetry.

I would like, with your permission, to tell you one episode most unforgettable among the others. The London winter of thirty years ago was something like a deep sea where dolphin or sharks leap, or like a certain part of a Hell in which death crawls from darkness to darkness. Excuse me for my bombastic metaphor, because with the coldness of shop-keepers this London did not appear to approve of my poetry. One night a poet friend led me to a late reception for another poet, where many people were found swimming from wave to wave in laughter or talk. My mind, dark and wretched, did not know how to join them. Like a nameless fish, its only art in smoking a cigarette, I cast my lonely small shadow on the floor from which merriment rose like a spring tide. I despised my own mind, and thought that I was a discredit to the fair name of Japanese, when I took notice of Hokusai's wonderful Fuji Mountain in colour-print, singing a song from between the rainbows on the wall written by reflection of the fire below. Then I thought that the mountain spoke to me: "Look at me, and rise! Look askance at the western people, and manifest the poet's glory! You must neither fear nor tremble! Take courage, I command you!" I felt at once my body vibrating with new life; all of a sudden I became talkative and lively. I was glad, for from that night the wry face of London began to smile. I smiled. My first book of poems appeared. How much I owe to Fuji Mountain! Fuji Mountain is my guardian angel, under whose protection my life as poet has been reclaiming itself. I am glad of it. I remember well how once in my boyhood I had been struck by the solemn beauty of the great sky. It was when I was eleven or twelve years old that, going down by a boat a little stream in my native village, we entered the river Kiso, and then the sea near Yokkaichi. I lay with my face upwards in the boat, and gated on the purplish sky. I said wonderingly: "What is the sky? How is it made? Oh, what a beautiful colour is the sky's! Who or what would there be behind it?" Many years have passed since I lay down again, not in the boat, but on a Californian hill that undulated like a sleeping tigress, and repeated my old wonder or adoration towards the sky. What was in the sky? There was the ringing echo of my question, but not the reply. My question about the sky I first asked in my boyhood is still unanswered to-day when I am near sixty. I stare at the sky through the glass-door facing my garden, when weather is bright with the clear air—in any season—and my mind is still troubled with the same old question. It was Wordsworth whose soul of old age leaped at seeing a rainbow as high as in his younger day. Who among the poets can escape from the psychology of his boyish mind? Our human knowledge loses its own function strangely when it faces nature. Ah, who can understand all of nature? We look up to it sometimes with fear, sometimes with wonder, and place before it our words of adoration.

My reverence towards the sea—mingled with fear—I am sure, would not be less than what I have to the sky. My being a poor sailor is always a merry topic among my intimate friends. At the time of my first American visit, I was already seasick before my steamer left Yokohama. There was in the ship an endless barking and kicking of Chinese gamblers by whom I was prisoned as a steerage passenger; but it is distinctly fresh in my memory, that I stole out onto the deck one midnight, when the crystalline sky in navy-blue was glittering with hundreds of stars, their beauty contested by the stars below. The stars below! The spray of the sea-water scattering over the deck from the right side at my feet! "Ah, what a sight of beauty, what a grandeur!" I exclaimed. The way before me, a boy student penniless but rich in dream, was almost black. I stood alone on the boundless expanse of water, under the darkness. I trembled against unknown future. Above my head there were the sparkling stars. I exclaimed then: Yes, I have only to fix my eyes on life's purpose that is permanent like a star—to live in light that is infinite!" On the deck at my feet there were the stars of spray. I exclaimed: "Yes I have only to cast my own self on life's board to make it glitter like spray. I have but to live in the moment's flaming life."

The thought of the Pacific Ocean brings me a thought of the Atlantic Ocean where I saw the memorable sight of icebergs. It was when I was twenty-eight years old that I left Liverpool towards Boston, where I expected to meet spring awakening amid flowers of March. The Northern Atlantic raged and stormed. When the steamer which had experienced the roughest possible voyage reached the middle of the ocean, it was obliged to stop in the night for many hours, warned by a whistle that rung wildly out from another trembling ship. In the morning I followed many other passengers, with no thought why they hurried about, onto the upper deck where, mercy on me, I was confronted with one huge iceberg glittering with the amazing sparkle of diamond. The cold monster of the restless ocean that gathered all the lights of water and sky in itself, burst into two pieces all at once, and with a king-like dignity they swum slowly away right and left. I thought that the dispute of grandeur in natural phenomena would certainly come to an end with this wonderful arch of the devils who celebrate their spiritual independence in the Northern sea. I could not help exclaiming then: "Oh, mighty nature, I kneel down to you!"

The voyage of the Indian Ocean also is one of my unforgettable experiences. I left Japan towards the end of October, and one month later reached Ceylon where all the plants and vegetables were found enjoying a life of relaxation, and pleased my passion for tropical unmorality. The steamer in which I embarked pushed its steady course between calm grey billows that reminded me of the tough skin of an elephant. I was delighted to see everything in the ship being gaily dressed in summer fashion. But the sea is not always a home for the sleepy god of peace, because a seven-headed dragon with violent languages pays a visit every four or five days, and plays the fearful tyrant. Among my bitter experiences on various seas, the storm that lay in ambush and frightened me on the homeward voyage, when my steamer was within a sailing distance of two days from Japan, is certainly the first thing I will remember for life. The ship was chased by maddening rain and blocked by vicious wind that carried away three boats from the deck. But a day comes when angry sea becomes a laughing water, wrath changes to a smile, and the menace of nature subsides into endearment.

I must write about waterfalls, after sea, and then valleys or ravines in association with waterfalls. I must write about mountains and trees also. First occurs to my mind the grand view of the Yosemite Valley, to which any human structure, a palace or tabernacle, however magnificent, cannot be more than a boy's whimsical endeavour. See the stone ramparts of the valley, all of them, that stand aloft or fly apart like a living animal! The rock that leans back is in shape of an old king who rests and communes with his soul. The rock rising perpendicularly a thousand feet high can be well compared with a philosopher who looks up and worships the burning stars. All the rocks here, ghostly taverns for the clouds, that, as I have written, refuse to let Fame and Gold sojourn, are apparently unapproachable, but they have certainly a tender aspect that talks smilingly! They welcome a storm with peaceful eyes, and their rugged hands touch a nameless flower with love. The feet of them are wrapped in trees and grasses fresh and luxuriant, the greenness of which will match with a gorge water where "an angel's ethereal shadow strays," while their proud heads lift to the dark-blue sky. This sky is the sky of which the Californians are so proud. The rocks are friends with rain, snow and wind, and even when washed by overwhelming flood, their lordly presence is inviolable. Around these august rocks, birds, bees, butterflies and a thousand unknown insects play. See how the Merced River runs through the heart of the Valley, with water that puts pearls to shame. This is the river by which wild grasses of all the seasons bury their whispering shadows, and trees comb their smoking hair. In this valley nature exhausts its own treasures.

I went there when I was twenty-one or two years old, that is to say, it was in an idyllic time of America before this reckless age of automobiles. I walked as I remember, by the mountain road, both sides of which were covered by white cedars and spruce trees, and with sequoias, kings of all the trees, and passed many a night in the open under their kindness. The night wind shook the leaves of trees and the stars in the sky to make them fall over my dream. What was the voice that called me in the dark? It was the soft lullaby of a valley stream by my bed among the hills of snow. Who ever thinks that snow is cold? It is not so unkind as it may appear to be.

It was about three o'clock in the afternoon that I came to the centre of the Yosemite Valley where by every step along the winding road the scenery diversified itself. Go down to the stream and taste how sweet the water is! Stop a moment and feel what a cool and bracing odour the valley trees diffuse! The beating sound of the water makes your ears prick up. That is the Bridal Veil Waterfall changing into a five-coloured rainbow under the golden flame of the sun that hurries westwards. Now you must prepare yourself not to become giddy and fall senseless from seeing El Capitan, the furious granite fortress, three thousand feet high. Where is there another natural wonder in the world, that can be compared with this astonishing power of God in one rock? When I approached Yosemite, it was already dark with many stars in the narrow sky! I felt with my eyes closed, that the roaring sound echoed from a cave of Hell a thousand miles away, or it was a shout of a god-scorning demon by the gate of Heaven. I looked up to the waterfall that hung down the sky in grey under the clouded moon. I exclaimed, awestruck by the angry threat of nature:

> A chariot rushes to an unknown hollow in wild triumph!
> Behold, a dragon reveals divinity in the ghostly-odorous sky of night—

Nay, the mighty sword of the Judgment Day blazes
down the Heaven to the gate of Hell!

Next morning the waterfall was found turning under the brilliant sunlight to white clouds gushing out, let me say, from Heaven's Eternal Court. I prayed to God with bending head, and felt that great silence in the voice of the water pierce my body. I raised my face again, giving thanks to the earth on which I could see such a glory in nature and kneel in fear-mixed joy. I thought then that man might be inferior to a bird. Birds sing a song and build their nests by the falling water, with no fear of its roaring incantation. What is the greatness of man who is proud of his intellect and passion? Man to whom sixty or seventy years are allotted at most, when facing nature, would seem merely odds and ends of human flesh.

The Niagara Fall comes in my mind with the Yosemite Valley. I had several occasions to call there at different seasons, in which my experience of it in the cold winter is most impressive. How can I forget this crystal palace of nature where the undaunted spirit of the fall finds its own way under the powerful encroachment of congelation! I will not oppose, however, to one who puts an emphasis on the summer beauty of it, particularly that under a moonlight. Charmed or bewitched by such a ghostly sight of the Niagara Fall in summer night, we find that nothing could seem simpler than to throw ourselves into the wonderful spray that sparkles in silver or gold. Again with this feeling I looked at and admired the Kegon Fall of Nikko one spring day of some years ago. How beautifully feminine the spirit of the water is! A man, weak of purpose and susceptible, might easily be destroyed by it! The spirit of the water is such a magician, good or bad, who melts and dissolves male spirits at will.

I often think that I began to understand nature with the grey-coloured aspect, that is, the negative beauty of it. When I was sixteen years old I began to read Basho, the 17th century

Hokku poet of Japan, who taught me the poetry of silence; my literary beginning was thus quite different from that of others who often began with sentimentalism toward a star or violet. It is told by a psychologist that the human understanding of colour advances from red and green to grey and black, from the showy to the settled. But as I said before, I began to look at nature first through the negative aspect of it, the appreciation of which makes me think that I must have been quite aged already when a mere boy. The beauty of showy colour in a red poppy or yellow buttercup began to move me when I lived with Joaquin Miller at his hillside cottage in California. I was then twenty years old. Therefore the development of my mind was the reverse of others.

My poetical work was begun with belief that I must appreciate nature with my emptied mind; I mean that I evolved poetically out of naturalism in which I strove to polish and brighten my soul to a transparent jewel or looking-glass, so that every fibre of nature could be reflected in it. But to-day, schooled in joy or pain, I cannot praise nature without a sense of criticism; I tend to think of it as standing face to face with my own life. Although not changed in my attitude of reverence, I cannot admire nature's dynamic beauty as before; my delight is in its still aspect. Facing nature on the further side of fifty, I surrender to silence. What I have learned at heavy expense through half a century, is but one word, "Silence."

And when I say that my adoration of nature, that is, my own poetry, begins and ends with Fuji Mountain, I am merely saying that I am a Japanese through and through.

The Adelphi, March 1935

The Candle-Light

In my boyhood reminiscences I appear selling candles at a neighbouring temple where an Okaicho is held. Okaicho is a festival for exhibiting a Buddha image which is particularly distinguished, and not commonly seen by the people. I was nine years old then, by invitation of the temple priest I took this holy role of sales-boy at a corner of the altar hall where votaries from ten miles around were choked by incense whirling in rings. The gold idol of Buddha placed in the centre of the hall looked down smilingly, as though on the point of speaking, over the human waves muttering prayers in unison. The offering money was thrown pell-mell at the image. As I remember, I was dressed like a gentleman in Haori and Hakama, ceremonial silken dress. Flattering myself that I had a lovely voice fitting for a singer, I raised it loudly: "Men and women of faith, make an offering of candles! One candle makes your soul clean. Ten candles insure your birth in Paradise. Buddha's promise is as sure as a rock!"

Thirty years later this candle-seller of an insignificant Japanese town is in London where he is fed and petted handsomely as somewhat of a poet. Released from a huge drawing-room with a Victorian ostentation that made him restless as he drank afternoon tea, heavy as bovril he passed one Sunday evening by Westminster Abbey, when the vesper-bell rang out. Being sensitive to religious things of any kind, he could not withhold himself from entering the Abbey in spite of his ignorance of Christianity, where under the ceiling that looked almost menacing he was but a pagan mouse losing his way. But candle-light already glowed, and, although not so modest and shy as that of Japanese candles, spoke doubtless the same celestial language; his mind was led straight way into composure. With many thanks to the candles which were kind in their hearts, though stout in appearance like Englishmen, he sat mingling with people who were waiting for the husky voice of a preacher. He would not object, he thought then, to taking the office of selling candles if he were asked to.

My reminiscence of Oxford is made delightful by candlelight and chimes. When my lecture was over at the hall of the Magdalen College, I withdrew into the common-room where, to the accompaniment of a wooden fire, the candles were humming a song of welcome. Shuffling off the mediaeval superiority of priests or magistrates, many dons surrounded me with all sorts of questions, wise or silly, which made the candles wink at me in sympathy with my situation. I had often read about the common-room talk as a speciality of Oxford; now I amused myself thinking that the calm perpetuity of Oxford was something invented by a Mrs. Grundy. However, this memorial convention, as far as I was concerned, broke off when the college chime reminded us of time, though not because of religious sobriety. I left the common-room with Robert Bridges who took me round to the chapel where the candles were burning, their reflection making the wooden panels at the sides shine. Not one student was found in the chapel. With a little smile of wisdom and satire, Bridges looked at me saying: "Students hate religion—don't you know it?" We bade the candles good-night, leaving them in nocturnal solitude to burn and shine alone. Even today I cannot help thinking that they are still burning beautiful and lonesome.

On my way home from London I stopped at Moscow for a week where I saw a forest-fire of candles, because the Kremlin, a sanctuary and spiritual fortress at that time, was commemorating the canonization of some saint. The sight of almost fantastic crowds of country pilgrims, sandal-footed, carrying cotton quilts on their backs for sleeping out, together with those audacious cupolas of gold, highly coloured walls and roofs, made me think at once of the savage extravagances where incongruity, warm and elemental, howled at civilization with intellectual restlessness, and abandoned itself even to mystery. But what I want to speak of here is the candles burning with motionless patience and disregard of time, that made the Kremlin a symbol of religious asceticism. Without knowledge as to what it was, I lost my own criticism against it; and in spite of myself, just like a Gorki or Stalins I had seen in the street, I traced a sacred cross on my breast. I was also impressed by smaller places of worship at each street, where attended by nuns black-hooded and black-robed, the little candles were burning. Although I was not sure whether I could pretend to be a pilgrim with a quilt on my back, I thought that I could easily return there in Moscow to a boy selling candles for the worshippers.

Living now in Japan, I sometimes visit Kyoto where, to please my mind, religious or poetical, I find my way towards the lonely Honen-in Temple nestled among the pinetrees, because I know that a few candles are kept burning there through the night. I wonder if there is anything like candle-light in an altar-room which, having no one before it, shines nobler and ghastlier. A few years ago when I climbed up Mount Koya, not so far from Osaka, where the monk Kobo of the early ninth century established his monastery, I walked alone late at night under the moonlight towards the inmost sanctuary along a path where a thousand Tombs stood under the huge cryptomerias. There was no human sound except my own footsteps echoing to the ghosts of departed souls. Received by candles burning sadly, I sat before the sanctuary deep in loneliness that numbed me almost to death. I do not remember how I left the place that night. What is distinct in my mind at present is that the candle-light at the sanctuary shone like a star beckoning to a stray soul.

Life and Letters, March 1935

The Sense of Existence

The tableland from Karuizawa to Komoro, three thousand feet above the sea, makes a large silent line, curved or straight like the sea in Korin's six-leaf screen, under the low ultramarine-coloured sky that plays a duet. Listening to this music with slow and simple rhythm, I felt myself to be in Heaven, or at least somewhere near it. . . . Who, being here, will not feel like a god or prince of the mythological age of Japan? Who will not feel that he is departing from the painful reality of earthly life? Who, to speak shortly, will not become a poet? Walking along this tableland, I send my fancy's birds to fly out over the great sea, and to smile, looking at their decorative beauty which belongs only to fallen petals. It is true that birds of fancy have gold and silver wings. . . . Oh, how these fancy birds mix together or separate, in the beauty of poetry!

Once, some years ago, when I visited this tableland and walked at leisure under the autumnal golden light in the afternoon, I happened to hear the voice of a cricket singing among the grasses. It was merely a little unpretentious voice; yet that voice was so great and strong, I felt, that it had the wide sky in ultramarine and the tableland covering hundreds of miles for its own. Then I thought that poetry, when it is true, should be like that cricket's voice; and then I was glad, thinking that I had discovered the secret road along which poets have to walk. We ourselves may not have more existence than a cricket, but if we could govern or hold sway over the sky and land with a cricket's little voice in adoration of Nature, our existence would certainly be greater.

The cricket does not belong to Japan alone. I have seen or

heard it in London and New York, but living in the material and stiff atmosphere that controls these western cities, people are apt to slight such a small natural phenomenon as the cricket. Though some poets of the West have sung about the cricket, in general they do not make a profitable theme out of it.

When I say that there is no difference between crickets and human beings, I do not mean to pull down the latter to the position of the former, but I mean to glorify the existence of the cricket as much as that of human beings. In truth our Japanese life, when the season moves from summer to autumn, will place us in a condition of accord with the existence of crickets and other insects. We would like to ask you if anything can exist without the faith that it is at the center of the world. Once I wrote of the sunflower:

> Thou art a lyric of thy soaring colour;
> Thy voicelessness of song is action.
> What absorption of thy life's meaning,
> Wonder of thy consciousness,—
> Mighty sense of thy existence!

Not only in the sunflower but also in the cricket, I find the "Mighty sense of its own existence." Of course, I look with full-hearted gratitude upon any phenomenon that strengthens my sense of existence, even when it is a minute thing, insignificant and trifling.

I have one more story to tell you in connexion with the cricket. I went to wash my hands once in the dead of night. When, after finishing what I wanted to do, I opened one or two storm-doors, the garden outside was as dark as pitch, and even the place where the pinetree and cryptomerias stood was not clear. I looked up to the sky where only one star shone between the darkest clouds; I looked down to the ground, and found there one little thing speaking a prayer toward the abstinent priestess keeping awake in the sky. Why, it was nothing but a cricket by the old well in the garden. When the lone star governed the wide sky, this little cricket, I found, was holding sway over the dark earth. I had never felt before, I confess, that the voice of the cricket could pronounce in such strong terms the great sense of its own existence.

Once some years ago I saw a great camphor-tree which adorned the garden of a friend, and praised the mighty sense of existence which I found in it. I thought then that this camphor-tree was more than tree, because it impressed me with something mysterious and divine. The tree, like King Harold of whom George Meredith sang, stood in the centre of the garden, spreading its kingly grandeur even beyond the boundary. Seeing that the house had been built so as not to be an obstruction to the tree, and that the perfection of the roof had been sacrificed at the place where the trunk stretched out its branches, I was struck with admiration, thinking that the builder of the house, my friend's father or his grandfather, was surely no small worshipper of trees. The camphor-tree was regarded here as a holy shrine where the spirit of Nature found safety. It goes without saying that a large straw rope with tufts of paper, a simple symbol of purity, girdled the tree. Then the house itself, with a large twenty-mat drawing-room where a beautiful hanging picture decorated the alcove at the left, seemed to be the warden's house of the shrine; that is to say, the camphor-tree. An autumnal frost had reddened the leaves of maple trees which were ready to fall into a little pond below in the garden; standing among these trees in their golden autumn clothes, I raised my admiring eyes to the camphor-tree, which stirred up my passion of tree-worshipping.

Where, except in Japan, can such a mysterious tree be found? There are in America a thousand big trees, which are absolutely unrivalled anywhere for size; the giant forest in the Mariposa county of California, for instance, is certainly a wonder in the kingdom of trees. But I do not find a mysterious existence in those trees, since they only impress us with their bigness—that is all. The question of mystery in trees, like anything else, should be solved through quality. When some Japanese trees give you the mysterious feeling that their form has been shaped in the pain of rain and wind for a thousand years, you do not think of them merely as trees, but as having an almost human existence. The camphor-tree is one of these which impress you with a strange spiritual life.

Perhaps I have talked too much of the tree, because what I wanted to say was about the cricket singing by that camphor-tree under the grasses. The voice was small, of course, but it proclaimed its own existence with as much dignity as the camphor-tree. To exist as an insect or as a big tree is a matter of chance. Let us believe in God who exhausted His best art for everything He created under the sun. Call me a cricket-small poet if you will! Who knows but that my song goes up to Heaven with a right equal to that of Milton or Dante?

The Spectator, 16 August 1935

Japanese Art

It was pleasant with a fine summer breeze at the top of Koya Mountain in Kii province, famous for its monastery, where I climbed a year ago; the breeze played a soft aerial melody in the pines ever fresh since the world began, and prepared an appropriate atmosphere for my seeing the priest Yeshin's work of Amitabha, there at the Treasure House. Unlike others who ascend the mountain for a religious purpose, thanksgiving or repentance, I went for art. Overflowing with joy, I examined the large hanging which was steeped in the "moonlight of Eternity," because it depicted Amitabha, the holy ghost of paradise followed by the three saints and twenty-five Bodhisattvas, welcoming departing souls from the earth below. Nearing in imagination the heavenly orchestra of flutes and pipes painted in the picture, I felt myself overcoming worldly cares and becoming detached from petty illusions for a greater freedom. I was dreaming a dream touched by reality but more intense and lofty.

Awakened by the thought that, in spite of my denial of a religious purpose in coming there, I was after all a religious pilgrim, I returned to the domain of art criticism and ventured to wonder why such a work lifted me to such a sweet and great mental experience, although it was evidently a temporary reaction. Not being a historical student, I do not know when Buddhism in Japan began to be coloured by pessimism; interpreted by an artist, however, as a synonym of beauty, pessimism became inseparable from Japanese life. I cannot help thanking the sculptors of the idols of Buddha or Boddhisattva which adorn the silent halls of the temples at Nara, because they explain that even at an early period, Japanese Buddhism was propagated through beauty. Supposing Nirvana, the cessation of individual existence, to be life's final desire, there is nothing more satisfactory than to contemplate it in an atmosphere where art is richest in beauty. Nothing in the art annals of the world, I daresay, is more perfect than the amalgamation of religion and art in the sculptures and paintings of Japanese temples. Moved by an imaginary melody, unworldly and mysterious, which these religious works diffuse, we lose ourselves, as with Yeshin's hanging of Amitabha, in a world of symbolic beauty where prayer is but the word of praise.

Although definitions of art may vary, no one would deny, I think, the value of harmony for its fundamental basis, because universal beauty, healthy and good, common to all people, is not a monstrosity or freak but a thing of symmetrical harmony in its expression. With what a harmonious arrangement Amitabha and Bodhisattvas are grouped in Yeshin's work! And then, what a distinguished centre of artistic expression is there in Amitabha! We know that the greater a work the more its inner light shines; and it does not give us, like an Academy painting of the present day, the impression that it is drawn for display. A western religious figure, a Christ or a Mother Mary who raises her hand and even smiles insinuatingly; is poles apart from a religious work like Yeshin's, for his work is but an artistic expression of austerities and a pictorial personification of prayer itself. We must pay great respect to the figure which appears not with the superficial pretension of a deliverer, but in an attitude of modesty, forgetting all surroundings in the concentration of its own thought. How meek Yeshin's Amitabha looks! I always think that, whether it be in painting or in the actual life of the human world, anything that exhausts itself not for display but for its own self-expression is beautiful, and qualifies for God's love. And there is nothing more appealing than a human being intent on the object of his purpose. When you see how eagerly children set their eyes on their balls or tops while playing, you cannot deny the artistic expression in their attitude. Hokusai, a town artist at the end of the Tokugawa regime, drew a thousand little scenes where a carpenter was busy with plane and saw, or a lantern maker with paste and paper, or a plasterer with trowel, and he humbly called them caricatures. Seeing there, however, a fervent artistic expression in those figures that are not abashed by the great art of the past, I owe many thanks to Hokusai for picking up his art from the human sweat and dust of mean streets. Not only Hokusai but many other artists of the so-called Ukiyoye school of Japan are artistic rag-pickers who lived in the lowly world but with their sincere eyes set upon the stars.

I once possessed several uncoloured proof-sheets of Utamaro's pictures called the "Silkworm Series," thin crumpled papers with the figures in black lines, which I bought from a second-hand bookshop on the shabby outskirts of Tokyo. Feeding my eyes on the supple and distinct lines that made the figures more beautiful because not disturbed by the encroachment of varied colours, I thought with gratitude that time was not altogether unkind in spite of its fame as a destroyer. Among the pictures there was one where a burning fire revealed the method of reeling raw silk, and many delicate threads hung down from the right hand of the woman at the loom, with such result that the artist stands unrivalled in line drawing through all ages. And I wondered why this female labourer looked so lovely till I thought that, concentrating on the work and not cutting a figure, she was seen to enjoy its progress. It is true that the art of Japan might have been like a green thicket without a rose, if without the appearance of the worldly studies of the Ukiyoye school where, through the virtue of real living in self-enjoyment, the figures, a half-naked barbarian of a back alley or a hired beauty behind a lacquered lattice, unconsciously assume a fundamental principle of higher art like Yeshin's Amitabha. There is no reason for those reports of daily life, though humbly depicted, to receive a lower estimation than a mountain or river in a six-fold screen.

Among the time-honoured subjects of Oriental painting the "Eight Views of Hsiao-hsiang" take precedence, for the shifting and changing of nature according to moon or rain is exhausted in the eight pieces. Harunobu of the Ukiyoye school said in his series, "Eight Views of the Drawing Room," that, since he had no real knowledge of this famous place in China, he was only too glad to find a suggestion of Hsiao-hsiang among the actualities of daily life. I cannot help regarding his attitude as much more true and worthy than that of the others who spent their art in a subject they only dreamed. Putting aside other things, this point alone makes Harunobu admirable, raising him to a higher plane to which only true artists have access. The world of his art, though small, is impressive with innocent and youthful people, who, ardently attached to their earthly lives, take such delight in their existence as to make us glad to share it equally.

Now leave art for a moment for nature in the garden where you will notice that even a little sun-plant grows to beautify itself and stretches up its body to the sun. You will find the pure undiluted spirit of art working within the aim of the sun-plant. I know no more impressive sight than that of a thing free and undaunted in its attitude of praising its own existence; and this attitude is art itself. God sees all his creations impartially: a towering tree or a creeping ant, a prime minister or a labourer hired by the day, —their intrinsic value is equal in nature when they absorb the joy of their existence. And there is no truer work for an artist than to report his existence. Musashi Miyamoto of the middle seventeenth century is a great artist, besides being an equally great swordsman whose heroism delights the populace through the cinema. Among his artistic legacy of only a few paintings, I find a work in black of two or three wild geese by marsh-reeds covered with snow. Like Yeshin's holy image at Koya Mountain or Hokusai's simple carpenter or lantern-maker, the wild-geese are here richly blessed by the ecstasy of their existence. What is art? It is nothing but a suggestion of something truer and nobler presented through the subjects in which the artist is interested. The priest Yeshin is not great just because he painted holy subjects. Again you cannot call Hokusai vulgar on account of his workmen of the slums. The art of both is great because of the sense of a blessed existence their subjects inspire.

There is no true art which has no direct relation to our own living. It has to cultivate our minds and enrich our souls. Suppose you say that the flowers of April know nothing of our hunger, even though they are as beautiful as a piece of brocade, and that the autumnal moon cannot do duty as an electric lamp, however brightly it may shine in the sky. Suppose again you ask how a picture of flowers of the moon can be directly related to our own living. I will answer: "What a stupid man you are not to recognise what a great influence natural phenomena, flowers or moon or what not, exert on us. I say that what is called love is immaterial, not a thing which we can hold with our hands or put in a measure; but anyone knows that love alone makes us understand life's eternity, and that its blessing is more real than that of a thing which you can see with the naked eye. Art is something like love or flowers or the moon, the mission of which is, with an intangible but real power, to develop our sense of living to something higher and nobler." The old art of Japan is in most cases quite far from so-called realism, even when it dips deep into the study of nature; accepting convention and therefore lacking in novelty of subject, the old artists still managed to bring out their personalities in artistic triumph. I always think, when I see a good specimen of the old art of Japan that it is fortunate for artists to know what kind of people they address, and what admiration or blame to expect from them, and that convention, when used with love, never restricts their vitality. Even though they sometimes seem fanciful or unreasonable, I am sure they will never offend us like the modern artists whose personal vanity glares under the name of individualism. To say that art should be the work of love or prayer is simple enough; but how many artists of the present time practise it? Japanese artists of olden days were true lovers of beauty before they were artists; as one prays to God in the same language day and night, they painted the same subject over and over, but with astonishing variety; what they aimed at was the true reality but not the appearance, the real execution but not the explanation of their themes. "Why, art depends, my old artist friend used to say, "on the artist's sensitiveness to the facts supplied to him, and upon his use of his hereditary and acquired methods of recording them, and upon his personal variation of those methods. No one dreams of praising the art of the sky itself, that is to say, the fact that the facts existed."

I cannot help wondering, in the first place, why the present artists of Japan in general should follow unconditionally after the realism of the West; this sad want of comprehension of fundamental principles makes me sceptical about the art of the future. Of course I have no objection to true realism which is an artistic means to an end, a touch of emphasis to bring out the inner spirit more clearly; but when it is not true realism but a superficial actuality not related to the ringing rhythm of spirituality, it would not be too much to say that it is a blasphemy against the artistic tradition of Japan, a true art bridging over the eternal and the ephemeral. Art that is merely ephemeral, however beautiful and elaborated it may be on the surface, has no more meaning than the fashion plate of the week. Since modern art is the mirror which reflects Japan's unqualified acceptance of the West, we cannot expect it to keep its old insularity. We have to recognize the general advance of modern artists in the handling of pigments as well as in exactness of delineation. But what true artistic value emanates from the fact that the branches and leaves of a tree are minutely drawn or the notes of a musical score on the piano (supposing we have a picture of a drawing room) look perfect as they are in reality? I think that such pictures are a waste of labour; at best they are the work of artisans and not of real artists.

But there are some artists of sterling merit who paint with love today—who form an artistic oasis where a pleasant breeze of new interpretation blows among the acquired traditional methods. When they paint a mountain or rugged coast in green or ultramarine, a pigment almost as rich as any western pigment, the effect they create, solid but beautifully delicate, would easily challenge any good work of the West. But generally speaking, our Japanese pigments want solidity; their excellence is in the quality, that is delicateness itself. Realising this undeniable fact, the old artists of Japan, when they drew something solid, hid or revealed themselves, according to the situation, in the magic of suggestive art in which the monkish black of India ink dominated. It was their own art to depart from seeming reality, and enter the inner spirit of it. Some ancient art critic talks about five colours of India ink, the spiritual beauty of which may surpass that of any western pigment. When the present artists of Japan cast away this India ink, they renounced their birthright. No real art comes out of the pigments themselves, however beautiful they are; there is nothing more dangerous in art than to abuse the materials. To see a large canvas thickly coated with pigments, a piece in which art is buried under piles of paint is sad indeed.

It is a pity that the present artists have lost the art of simplicity which our old artists discovered at the sacrifice of emotional expression. True art which becomes an adornment to human life, is born from simplicity, the symbol of reality. Why should we be thankful for art if you cannot draw a dream from it? As we say that a simple dream is the most beautiful, we can say that art, when it is simple, pleases us most, because it hypnotises us into a twilight land of ghosts. The best works of the old art of Japan, from the folding screens of Yeitoku or Sanraku to the colour prints of Harunobu or Buncho, keep themselves closely to this canon of simplicity. Admitting that art should adhere to the psychology of the time, I would be only too glad if the present art of Japan would advance into a heterogeneous beauty built on the law of simplicity.

My friend, a well-known expert on Japanese music, surprised me the other day when he began:

"Did you ever see the picture of a waterfall by Wang Wei of the early T'ang dynasty at the Chijaku-in Temple in Kyoto? No? Very well! it is a horizontal piece not so significant in its size as in its content and remarkable meaning. The brush of an artist, little as it is, can be called an instrument of magic when it makes the infinity of space ring rhythmically at its touch, heavy or light. According to a western dictum, the music of a picture is sweeter because it is unheard. This work of Wang Wei illustrates remarkably well the point I am now speaking of. You should see it at the first opportunity when you go to Kyoto again. There are a few varied parallel lines drawn diagonally in the centre of the canvas,—that is a huge waterfall between crags, whether it is a real sketch or an imaginary creation. It is no exaggeration to say that without apparent beginning or end, the lines bridge the infinity of space. Here subtilty exhausts itself. And how happy I am that such a picture endorses my opinions about music, because music when at its best in melody, should respond to the infinity of time which vibrate in the air inaudibly. I thank God, all the arts are one after all."

This verbal essay on rhythmic Infinity renewed at once my interest in the subject, and made me think about Togan's sliding screens of eight panels at Marquis Kuroda's home; the subject is plum-blossoms and crows, and space is treated in a manner, I think, not below that of the work of Wang Wei which my friend pointed out. Running diagonally through the great canvas covered with brilliant yet quiet gold, the branches of the plum-tree are drawn in black and remind me of the spare frame of a Zen priest who has the fire of perception burning within. A botanical forerunner of the season, the plum-tree depicted in the work is a symbol of indomitable spirit unyielding in the cold of early spring; this symbol suggests something older and larger than art, because as a temporary form of reality it causes the rhythm of the space, the undrawn part of the work, to vibrate. It is natural that the aerial melody of that space is grave, since it solemnly obeys a beckoning hand in the branches. Togan's lines and dots, therefore, are but a suggestion and a hint that bring out a far greater meaning than that of a mere revival of the plum-tree.

In the works drawn by Dasoku, at the Yotoku-in temple, Kyoto, the great Zen priests, Dharma, Tokusan and Rinzai, loom up with the whole sky at their backs. Putting aside the value of the pictures that, as a figure study, would easily lead many others, see how the huge space in the undrawn part whispers a mystery of rhythmic Infinity to the priests deep in meditation! Unlike that of Togan's screens the space of these religious portraits is melodious in a well-composed soft voice, performing a natural duet with the priests in the foreground whose voices have lost their sharpness. To say that the portraits are equal to the space, would be an over-estimation of the former, because all artists should be sensible enough to know that their crafts, however admirable, are trifles compared to Infinity. The painted part of any picture is only valuable as a pictorial talisman; and this talisman, when it properly exerts its own magic under the blessing of the undrawn part, becomes great with undying glory. Above all else the integrity of space should be protected in a painting, and not one line or one dot can be slovenly lest it damage the beauty or foolishly disturb the rhythm.

I have often before spoken of this in the works of Sotatsu and Korin, and exclaimed, "What a wonder of space! And what a wonderful handling of the brush!" One is amazed at the boundlessness of space, when he sees Sotatsu's famous screen of the "Wind-God and Thunder-God" at the Kenninji temple, Kyoto, where the painted figures fly furiously above the fretful earth spinning far below. The work is but a mighty battle between pictorial silence and pictorial voice. For Korin's screens of the iris flower, once an heirloom of the Honganji temple of Kyoto, I admired the manner of the artist that he did not spoil the huge space in the background with a bird or butterfly; if Korin had not been as great as he was, he would have been afraid to hear the ringing music of space in its entirety. The canvas, whether it be silk or paper, whether it be picture or hanging scroll, is a battlefield for the artist where reality and unreality, the painted part and the unpainted part, contest on even ground. It is a foolish artist who thinks that his work begins and ends with his painting brush. And your eyesight may be enough to see the painted part of a picture; but your whole body should be responsible for the real appreciation of the Infinity that the unpainted part suggests. "That is the point for the musician too," my musician friend exclaimed. "I would call it real music when it appeals not alone to your ear but to your whole body from head to foot. But it is sad to say that there is seldom such great music. Besides, people hear and understand music only through its sound."

This final remark made me recall the reply of Beethoven, when he was once asked what was great in music, "No music, Sir," he said. I saw the other night the solo dance of Kikugoro, a Kabuki actor, in the piece called "Yasuna." Yasuna is a youth mad because of unrequited love; personified by Kikugoro, Yasuna moved about the stage in the fashion of a sleep-walker, according to the text, haunted by the shadowy image of his sweetheart among the rapeseed blossoms and butterflies. I said "moved" purposely because he did not dance at all; if he danced, it was the dance of a soul who reduced, as far as dancing allows, all the actions to stillness where, like a poised fish, he kept an aerial balance. Although it was a spectacular performance accompanied by *Samisen* music and song, I felt myself to be in a silent hall where physical expression was considered vulgar. The dancer raised his hands and feet, and turned his face right and left enigmatically in a way that only people familiar with dancing vocabulary would be able to read. I know that, although not a representation of the Japanese dance, this "Yasuna" is like the others in the vital point that physical movement is compressed inwardly in the interest of artistic economy.

Recalling Harold Kreutzberg's madman which I saw some time ago on the Japanese stage, I cannot help thinking about the difference between these two dances, Japanese and German. Since this ultramodern German attempted to interpret a madman's psychology realistically, he had his own license for physical movement, however unstable and wild. How speedily his movement shifted and changed! I do not think I am mistaken in saying that, in general, the western dance has its artistic focus in speed which outwardly becomes loose and frayed. Though I have no mind to censure it as an acrobatic feat, western dancing is nothing if not danced with the whole body whose functions, every one of them, respond to one another in leaping harmony. We Japanese are, let me say, backward in the expression of this modern movement for in "Yasuna," whether the dancer steps fast or slow his heels keep close to the floor, and do not allow his movement to spread out from his centre of gravity which is in his body. Therefore even as a madman, Kikugoro's Yasuna, unlike the madman of Kreutzberg, is able, as it seems, to concentrate and to control his mind and body.

The chief value of a Japanese painting will be found in its lines, the art of Japanese dancing is measured by the forms of the lines, straight or curved, delicate or heavy, gross or light, which the dancer draws with his body. If western dancing is not careless about the lines, we find it, I believe, mainly in the form that extends and spreads outwardly in action; on the contrary, our dances are at their best when the lines enjoy the solstice of negation. It is natural that, as in the case of "Yasuna" our dancing is monotonous with the monotony which purposely sacrifices variety. And it is true that, not only with dancing but with all the other matters of art, this monotony is a fundamental characteristic of the Orient, at least, of Japan.

It is not too much to say that all our artists are like tight rope-walkers, moving safely or unsafely on the single silver wire of the monotony of Japanese life. If you doubt my word, see Korin's screens of sea-waves undulating in silent monotony, where the sea seems controlled by the magic of this Japanese Prospero of art and one could easily cross like Ferdinand with dry clothing. Or see Taiga-do's hanging picture of nature where mountain over mountain and water over water are pictured vertically in monotonous lines. Your mind, if it is appreciative, will be mesmerised by those lines into a trance where all actions stop; but if you are a hard-headed and unappreciative person, Taiga-do's monotonous mountains in the picture will appeal to you only as a meaningless pile of Chinese yams. And see again Kikugoro's dance of "Yasuna," his silken sleeve "disordered by a mad wind of love!"

Occasionally there are times when the mental pressure of the monotony of life or art becomes unbearable, and I want to find an escape from it. At such moments the following passages come to my mind: "A man went to a Zen priest and disturbed his meditation with complaint. He said: 'I am miserable because I am poor. I am miserable because I am ill in health. I am miserable because I am old.' The priest replied: 'If you are poor, you should live in poverty. If you are ill in health, you should live in ill health. If you are old you should live in old age. Then you will be happy.'"

No good swimmer struggles against the tide. One must go to darkness for the light of day; and in evanescence the truth of eternity shall be found. Call it a half truth if you will; I know that the half moon will soon be full. And if you like, your question of monotony shall be solved through the blessing of assimilation. I say to you, "Live in monotony, and forget it!"

It is a cold truth that all the phenomena of the world, the sun and the moon and stars, move about, grow or die, on the eternal principle of monotony. Even the tiniest ants in a back yard are busy in their harvest, ruled by that principle which they observe. If western people seek complex colour and action in life and set their eye on forward movement, they should be reminded of our Japanese way, represented in Kikugoro's "Yasuna," where our heels do not leave the floor and our minds do not break away from mental centre of gravity.

Besides, you would feel no monotony, I am sure, if like Korin or Taiga-do, you painted sea-waves or even mountains of Chinese yams. And again if you dance "Yasuna" like Kikugoro, I do not see why you should feel monotony. The most important issue is how to become a Korin or Taiga-do or a Kikugoro.

My artist friend interested me when he talked about Chinese ink-sticks; he told me of a special kind called "Ch'ing-chu-Mo," meaning "ink-stick of the Whale Pillar." The emperor of the Wan-li era, the story says, dreamed one night that a whale coiled around the pillar of the Imperial chamber; proclaiming it an auspicious omen, the emperor bade the court ink-stick maker, Cheng-Tai-Yueh, to symbolise the dream in his trade. This august origin, I am happy to say, protects itself even today against degeneration, because, when rubbed on the slab, it shines in purple. "Such purplish colour glittering from within," my friend exclaimed. "It is one colour but inwardly has many colours, which mingle into purple, and lure us into rapture."

Then he told me how he wraps the Ch'ing-Chu-Mo, being a happy owner of it, with the *moxa* which keeps it from getting too dry or too damp; as the culmination of his talk, the following anecdote pleased me. One summer morning some years ago, when his spirit was so moved, he brought out a large slab with his beloved ink-stick, Ch'ing-Chu-Mo, then called out to one of his students to make ink for a work that already whirled in his mind. The student withdrew with them, the slab and ink-stick together, into the next room. My friend sat upright to compose his mind, like an ancient warrior in the moment before a final combat, smelling the perfume of incense which rose from the alcove. After a little while he called his student loudly over the screens, asking if the ink was not yet rubbed. Responding to his voice, the young fellow appeared with the slab where in the hollow part the black ink overflowed. My friend only stared at the student in amazement, struck dumb, because he wanted just a little of the fresh ink. As an artistic acolyte, the student did not know what this Ch'ing-Chu-Mo meant to his master. "A few teaspoonfuls of ink are enough for one work," my friend said, because one drop of it makes a mountain peak and another a crow in the sky. We Orientals cannot erase or change our first stroke like the artists of the West, for the first brush mark is also the last and final." Then he exclaimed after a moment of amusing hesitation: "Beside, this ink cost me one hundred pounds. Thanks to my student I lost ten pounds at least on that morning!"

This story of my friend reminds me at once of the current phrase, "Be saving of ink as with gold!" It goes without saying that not only in ink but in other things artistic magic can be performed with economy. A mind worth ten thousand pounds is more important than an ink-stick worth one hundred pounds. One must admit, however, that only Ch'ing-Chu-Mo can interpret a ten thousand pound artistic mind. To a westerner who might take our ink-stick for a piece of charcoal, it would be surprising to know how costly it is even in material value. There are many people of course both in Japan and China who see only black in ink-stick, not the various colours it reveals when at its best, because art has nothing to do with an unappreciative mind. If there is one mysterious thing in the world, it is art. Again how mysterious is our ink-stick!

We have a word we fondly use, Ko-tan meaning "Plain and Naive," although literally it is "Withered and Light." This word may well be applied to *sumiye*—an art like winter sunlight concealing tenderness within the lonely surface, which withdraws backwards to its original start-point where differentiation of colours is not yet dreamed of. Resolving itself into a line or dot, the painting in black represents expression brooding in anticipation or reminiscence. If one knows that he cannot draw a line and dot so strongly in red or green as in black, the value of ink-stick in art is far more fundamental and definite. Therefore it is not too much to say that our Oriental art on paper or silk reaches its climax in ink painting.

Let me quote the following poem which I call "A Theory:"

> Let me teach you how to draw a picture.
> First of all, put one circle on the upper part of a paper
> . . .
> That is Eternity. You may call it
> Sun or moon, if you will. Then group
> Many a triangle in any but interesting ways.
> These are mountain-ranges, resting shapes.
> Underneath, parallel lines . . . these mean a river—
> an action.
> However varied the forms of nature may be,
> They are, after all, but circle, triangle and parallel
> lines.

When the Oriental artist using only black draws nature in the final aspect of dissolving itself into circle, triangle and parallel lines, I do not think him in the babyhood of art, because, leaving all else to suggestion, he sticks to inevitability, rich in the essence of Ko-tan, plain and naive. I always believe that art at best expresses only two-thirds of its meaning leaving the other third to the co-operation of the appreciators. And again it is in the appreciator's jurisdiction to change black in his mind into any other colour, if he will, to admire the work in his own way, since black is unlike other specific colours and is neutral in temperament.

Of course Oriental art of the Ko-tan qualification is like a Ch'ing Chu-Mo with inner gleams or again like a winter sunlight,—not dry and tired. It is interesting to trace painting in black to its first use in China by a recluse in the forests or a hermit in a cave, who through life's simplification sought the way of purification, and established the world of solitude where light shines within. I have wasted many words on Ch'ing-Chu-

Mo and on monochrome painting because I think that life's dissolution into a line or a dot means a rejuvenation that is salvation.

The annals of Japanese art are a great galaxy including Sesshu, Tannyu, Koyetsu, Korin, Yeitoku, Sanraku, Matabei, Hogai, Gaho and many others. Although the battle fields of those artists were limited to sheets of paper or silk, the records they left, the rainbows they drew with a few drops of pigment, are more wonderful in undying beauty than the memories of soldiers famous for drawing swords and blood in history. With a great sense of joy I trace back the history of Japanese art to the early Heian period of the ninth century when Saicho and Kukai, outstanding figures of the priesthood who studied in China, propagated religion and art simultaneously; it would be truer to say that they taught religion through art. Their efforts, I think, prove that these two things are after all the same. The appearance of Kanaoka Kose was highly significant, because like the *Uta* poets in "Kokin-shu" or Ancient and Modern Poems of the tenth century, Kanaoka broke away at once from Chinese imitation and established a national sentiment and ideal in art. But the cultural history of Japan in the past is the flowing or ebbing tide of Chinese influence. When the art of picture scrolls which flourished in the early twelfth century was replaced by the so-called Art of Higashiyama Hill (Kyoto) in which the simple and thrifty spirit of the time was endorsed by the Zen philosophy of China, the alien influence spread over into Japan. This Chinese influence was again driven back when great masters like Koyetsu, Sotatsu and then Korin entered the artistic world of the seventeenth century. And with the gradual development of Ukiyoye in painting and print, a genre treating the manners and customs of the lower classes became the final property of the Japanese people.

All things considered, I think that the greatest worth of our Oriental art is to be found in the poetical atmosphere of becoming one with nature. "What a delightful shape," we say, looking up at a summer cloud in the sky. "How beautiful it is," we think, seeing a rose in the garden. Such is the moment when, through the appreciation of a single phenomenon, cloud or rose, we unconsciously touch and understand all the phenomena of nature; then it is not a mere question of cloud and rose, because they reveal their lives as part of all nature. Our sense of beauty, varied of course according to individual gift and training, always sleeps until nature enters our vision; human existence becomes clearer by contrast with nature. We might be lords of the creation with all the knowledge necessary to seek beauty in it; but when lacking in sensibility, our human faculties would not properly work to make life vivid. We must try our utmost to keep our souls in perfect safety so that no kind of corruption may encroach or play wicked mischief with them.

Since art is a natural outcome of our human desire, the expression of painting in treatment as well as in subject varies, according to the nature of the people and the country; so the painting of Japan cannot be uniform, of course, with that of the western countries. If the latter places emphasis on the temporal life of human beings and, unlike our old painting, conveys only seldom the poetical conception of the extra-territorial kingdom of self-effacement—an amalgamation of nature and man—that is because the artistic requirement of the West is different from that of the East. Without criticising the Western understanding of nature, or doubting the sincerity of it, I wish to say that Westerners hardly agree with us in the belief that man is merely a part of pure nature, a being congealed from the vital breath of nature. We, Orientals, think that human beings are built with the same elements as those of the wind that blows in the sky, or of the rain falling to the ground, or of cloud and haze swimming in air; therefore we can enter easily into a proper comprehension of nature, and our consolidation with it is only natural. We make subjects treating nature an essential part of painting.

People of the West would hardly understand our conception of nature, the basis of which is adoration but not criticism. When we communicate with nature by gazing on her beauty, we know that our human existence becomes clearer than before, because of a self-realisation that is achieved unconsciously. The blessed kingdom of self-effacement admits only him who becomes one with nature; he is intoxicated by his own happiness. If he is an artist, he tells about it on paper or silk, with Indian ink or pigments; and if he is a poet, he sings about the joy of the kingdom in words.

Because we stress the spiritual beauty of everything, we often slight the structural development which is to us a more or less superficial matter. Certainly it is no apology for a lack of objective description when our artists talk so much about "pictures of spirit." There are many works of old and new artistic criticism in the Orient, among which we prize "Kiun Seido" or Living Inner Motif as the first and last qualification; however perfect in technical arrangement, a work is nothing to us if it does not suggest a spiritual beauty.

The Calcutta Review, December 1935

Japanese Poetry

I was a poor tramp who chopped wood for a breakfast, when I once wandered, some forty years ago, over mountains and rivers along the Pacific coast of America. It was penniless travelling with no set number of miles to walk each day, a beggar's journey unrestrained and free, with nothing under the sun to fear. I was a stranger in a strange land and lonely without a home but I depended on my youth and healthy body, always ready when I found no roof to cover me, to pass the night in the open air. How many times I regarded a stone under a tree as a warm bed!

It was in early May when, on the way to Yosemite Valley, I had to sleep one night at the foot of a mountain, as a Japanese phrase goes, pillowed on a stream. I gathered grasses and small stones, broke off the branches of a tree near-by, putting them on the blanket which covered me, because on account of its lightness I could not compose my mind to sleep. As the night advanced, the voice of the stream grew so clear and dreary that my soul, whose existence I felt, became more distinct, was bitten through by it; the world was pitch dark. Lying in the darkness, my eyes grew wider and wider; after looking about the trees for a moment, they left the earth and gazed up at the sky, rising higher and higher to a spot where, beside a cloud black and precipitous like a cliff, one brilliant star shone like a diamond. I myself and the star in the high sky held the immeasurable distance between; there was nothing to interrupt the space. I alone gazed up at the star. And the star gazed down, I felt, on me lying on the ground by the stream. This confronting of the midnight in the lonely valley made me shudder for its sublimity merged into ghastliness.

But gradually I grew to feel like a silent priest praying in the temple, as I recalled the Hokku poem of Rotsu, the beggar poet of three hundred years ago,

> The wet-month night is dark!
> Finding one star in the sky,
> Oh, how I prayed to it, how I prayed!

My star in the high heaven now appeared to respond kindly to me, the sublimity that made me afraid changed softly and the ghastliness of the midnight began to smile endearingly. Relieved of fear and blessed by nature's warm breath, I slowly entered into peaceful sleep. That night I felt most acutely that, like Rotsu who sat flat on the ground like a beggar, we should raise our heads from the low ground towards nature and worship it. The lower the ground the greater nature becomes.

Because we Japanese sit down on the floor, low to the ground as I was during my penniless journey in America, we are more fortunate than westerners in an amalgamation with nature; without the sense of worship that is offered from the humblest place, one cannot enter nature's inmost shrine and receive from it the last benediction. Westerners who stand erect or sit on chairs will see nature upward from paunch to head; but they miss seeing that the sweetest things are performed close to the ground; these things the man who sits humbly down will see better.

> It is the sitting man's right, the scrutiny of littleness, in flower-petals,
> It is the sitting man's right to flit with the baby butterflies from grass to grass,
> It is the sitting man's right not the standing man's, to see nature's loins or feet.
> Praised be the man who sits down, he lives many feet nearer the ground,—
> No need to bend his body for thanking God or

praising the moon in a pond!

I seldom see western painting or read western poetry without feeling that they are the works of man standing erect rather to criticise than to pray; rather to explain than to adore. If westerners are lacking in natural piety, they should remind themselves of their manner when they pray to God before they go to sleep. It is the virtue of a man sitting down to see level with the ground where, if the time is spring, flower-petals fall to make a fabric in dappled white. I am second to none in recognizing the high standard of English poetry, perhaps the highest in the world; the galaxy of the past masters almost blinds me with its splendour. Putting ceremony aside, however, I will say that, if I cannot give myself to those masters body and mind, it is not from a difference of education and environment but from a difference of attitude towards nature. On the other hand how it doubles my pleasure to find in English poetry an equal though infrequent worship of nature, humble and pious, as when Wordsworth looked up to the rainbow which made his heart leap up or John Keats to the star in his last sonnet.

Fearful in the anticipation of approaching death, Keats left an English port for Italy; it was on the evening of the 28th of February, 1821, that the young poet gazed from the deck low down on the sea up to the star where beauty bewitched him. His attitude was more complicated than Rotsu's pure and simple in a beggar's fashion, because his natural adoration was mixed with the love agony of life's last moment. But who will doubt their affinity—man sitting down but with their heads raised upwards?

I would take a western visitor to the tea-ceremony house, if he wants to see something distinctively Japanese, and make him stand on a garden-path of stepping stones and listen to my words: "This little passage is called *Roji*, a very styx where you should forget the physical world and enter into self-reflection." I know that my foreign friend would look about the garden enclosing the house with leaves, green or dark; pointing to a spot where an old tree is particularly grey with the age of a thousand years, I might say to him: "Do you know what is called the blessing of silence? We, Orientals, are happy to find the climax of poetry in solitude. Led by a faint soft light of loneliness, we would slowly approach an aesthetic hall of rapture, an ecstatic den of beauty, a holy sanctum of idealism. Whatever you call it, the name is nothing. I only know that this is the place where Infinity dwells in solitude and one's individuality, simple and true, does perfectly "saturate with the soul of the universe." Then the granite lantern that squats like a saint or poet will inspire me to speak further: "There in the inmost heart of the lantern is a beacon light that shines upon truth, teaching us how to cross the sea of the world, mad and angry, or how to get clear of the dust of life's ruin. It will teach us how to create an atmosphere, pure and true, in which a silent prayer leads us into the Teaism of Japan."

To my western friend I will not fail to explain how near the ground the floor of the tea-house is made, so that we can look up at nature humbly from below. And when he notices the eaves of the house with their long slope, I will say to him: "We have to thank the darkness in the house, because it facilitates the concentration of our thoughts or fancies."

Then I lead him within the house, and ask him to sit down on the matted floor, cold and damp; that may be unpleasant but I am sure he will not contradict me if I say that he should close his eyes in reverie. What would he answer me, if I should say to him: "Pray, let me hear what you think about the rapturous world, sweet and quiet, which we hope to create here! I should like to know what effect the mystery of meditation works on your soul. Are you already purified, are you blessed by all freedom?" My friend, the visitor from the western country, would smile a little without a word; I know that his smile means nothing definite. Except for a few men whose natural gifts are particularly sympathetic to the aestheticism of the

East, ordinary westerners in sack-coats may not understand my words. Of course the fault is not with them, because our conception that art reaches its highest point of simplicity when nature and life amalgamate into one, is something beyond their understanding, and Teaism, a philosophy practised in a tiny house with kettle and bowls, is one of the expressions which proves that the old culture is still living with the undying fire in the present time.

A most interesting story is found in an old book, concerning Lord Hidetsugu, a Shogun and tea-master, who once invited a few friends, like-minded in worshipping at the altar of boiling kettle, for tea at early dawn. All of them were famous tea-votaries of the day. The season was April, the day the twentieth, when the cherry blossoms, though hesitating to fall down, already suggested that Spring had grown old. Outside the tea-house, the breezes, still in the gown of night, brushed the dewdrops under the eaves, while the dusky souls of night grouped themselves in battle array in the garden trees before a final retreat. Within, silence reigned over the house where no light was lighted; but soon the kettle began to boil, singing an old melody that pleased the guests who looked forward to the appearance of the host. Shogun Hidetsugu was so slow, the guests were almost tired of waiting, when, instead of the host, the Ariake-no-Tsuki, the faint light of the falling moon at early dawn, slid into the room like a guest arrived too late. All the guests followed in the moon's footprint towards a little alcove, where the light stopped on the *shikishi* paper tablet, on which the following Uta poem was written:

> Where a cuckoo a-singing swayed,
> I raised my face, alas, to see
> The Ariake-no-Tsuki only remaining.

The guests, all at once, looked at one another with minds for the first time, leaping to the knowledge that the invitation of the august lord meant the introduction of the poem; they exclaimed but silently: "Oh, how admirable is the taste of his lordship!"

The story stops here. I am not told whether or not the Shogun appeared on the scene, or how the tea-ceremony at early dawn ended; but that is not the important point, because the central value of the story is in the artistic attitude of Hidetsugu which blossomed mysteriously out of Teaism. Because he created a particular atmosphere highly fitting his artistic purpose, Hidetsugu was a poet not of words but of an action, aesthetically minute and fastidious, fermented from the culture at the final moment of distillation. No one would object, I am sure, if I say that I do not know a sweeter, a more beautiful way than what the Shogun selected for the introduction of the poem. I would say again that I do not know a more beautiful, a sweeter situation than that which the guests found apparently by accident for the appreciation of it. The Shogun was fortunate in having guests whose aesthetic minds were rightly responsive; with the proper action of the moon as a scene-shifter, I should say the host and guests completed a stage scene in the tea-house most poetically.

I have no mind to criticise the western countries because they value quantity more than quality: I know that they often become disjointed and confused, because of ignorance or neglect in adjusting and regulating life and nature: matters, when left alone, are apt to grow untidy. If we, Orientals, have anything to teach the western people, it should be the lesson of selection or simplification. The philosophy that developed in a tea-ceremony house, Teaism in one word, centres in the virtue of silence which perfects itself only in solitude; it is simple enough to say that we see the major in a minor, the universe in a dewdrop, but only one with a mind transcending space and time, would be able to practise this way of viewing life. If the tea-masters of Japan listen to a philosophy or sermon in a tea-bowl but not to a social talk as from a western cup, it is not too much to say that they have specialised in the perfection of self-adjustment. The tea-ceremony house is a structural trifle, but its meaning in existence, at least to me, is as great as Westminster Abbey or Notre Dame. Do you laugh at me as an irresponsible freak?

I know almost nothing about the rituals of the tea-ceremony. Supposing I lead my foreign friend to a tea-house, I do not mean to dwell on the technical exposition of the ceremony, because my chief interest is to find there a spiritual extra-territoriality where life and death are one, being delivered from the restrictions of the physical world. If my friend from the west is rich in poetical conception, I am sure that my standpoint will not be altogether alien to him, and he will join me in the conjuring-up of Infinity. Although the Teaism of Japan is distinctly characteristic of our home, native in development, it is not without universal elements because art, when it is true, knows neither the east nor the west. I am not disappointed in the present westerners, if they do not understand this particular cult of tea-drinking. Hope for the future makes me continue talking of its aesthetic value.

Let me tell you one more story concerning a morning glory. Two great figures of the sixteenth century, Rikyu, a tea-master, and Taiko Hideyoshi, a mighty war Lord, are in the story, the former as a cultivator of the flower, and the latter as one burning with a desire to see it. It goes without saying that the morning glory was the rarest of things at that time. When Taiko once accepted Rikyu's invitation for a morning tea, his mind was gladdened more by the anticipation of the flower than the tea itself; finding none of the morning glories, however, on his arrival at Rikyu's tea-house, Taiko was displeased and asked him rudely: "Rikyu, where is the morning glory?—You are so proud of it, I understand." Rikyu answered nothing to him. But the displeased Lord followed after the great tea-master into the house, where he sat, and, turning his face towards the alcove, doubted his eyesight when he saw a tender vine of morning glory with a flower-cup smiling like a bit of rainbow that had forgotten to disappear. The story should stop here without dwelling on Taiko's perplexity as to what to do about his hastily made accusation, or upon the recognition of his defeat in an artistic combat with the tea-master. Of course the most important point of the story is that Rikyu destroyed all the other morning glories on that morning, and created a highly distinguished situation for the one that remained. I am sure that, like a last warrior left upon the field, Rikyu's morning glory in the dark alcove must have appeared in tragic beauty, full of gratitude for the sacrifice of its compatriots.

This attitude of Rikyu in which he destroyed ninety-nine morning glories out of one hundred, is that of artists, who protected their own art with self-mortification that was almost religious. One who lives in solitude in a psychological climax, of mind in which all passions subside, would be able to enjoy the lonely song of a soloist. That was, in Rikyu's case, a morning glory solitary in the alcove where dusks gather even in the daytime. What an abstract mystery, what a dream-like beauty in it! There is nothing but solitude that preserves perfectly the spiritual integrity of one's self. When we find that the personalities of poets, artists and tea-masters, great in the old artistic annals of Japan, are solid and rich, that is simply because, as soloists, they sent their silver-clear songs of existence over the wild expanse of Eternity.

It is not too much to say that, if in poetry or painting or tea-ceremony we cease to be soloists, we are already doomed to artistic ruin. Oh, how it would be, like a lost homeless people, to wander about the western countries for cultural scraps! We may be sure that if we once become artistic vagabonds, it will be almost impossible for us to recover the lost kingdom. Therefore now, more than in any former time, the maintenance of Teaism is most momentous for us, because, as we well know, heterogeneous multiplicity is raising a wild battle-cry and assaulting the lone castle of oneness.

From olden times in the west the words, the "beautiful

madman," have been accepted even with a touch of superstition. Whether or not laurel leaves are edible it is often said that a poet, when he is great, is a man growing mad because of them. Shelley was pointed out as an example of this. But the Japanese opinion of a great poet differs because we think he should spit out the laurel leaves, supposing he had been eating them, and return to normality. A poet is to us not a man who expresses his madness outwardly, but one who keeps it within, if he has it, and settles his soul in solitude. I say that our ideal poet reaches the high-water-mark of his art in the state of impersonality, slipping out of the company of Intellect or Individuality, and he takes shelter in abandonment where life shows its natural aspect.

I have often talked about the enchantment of impersonality, because it seems to me the original state of being in which there is no difference between life and art, and nakedness is praised for its own sake. It is a blessed condition when indulging in the leisure of platitudes, even a great poet forgets his tongue in self-enjoyment, and a few words suffice, although others take them for riddles or childish babble. In Japan there is no one like a poet for depending on the sympathy of his friends, because that alone can make his imperfection perfect. Again there is no poetry in the world like Japanese poems, isolated and disconnected which call pathetically for the rescue of a reader's understanding.

Now I recall, on a day almost forty years ago, a Californian hillside crouching in lion fashion but beautifully clothed with golden buttercups and poppies, where I lived with meadow larks. The time was spring when, according to Browning, God was in heaven and all was right with the world; the morning was at nine, not seven as in his song but, in agreement with it, the hill-side was dew-pearled. There was a long narrow wooden bridge over the grasses, connecting the public road and my little cottage which nestled in the rose bushes; for a gate two rough-planed wooden posts stood at the end of the bridge.

That particular morning when an American lady friend called on me, she found that one long diamond string of a spider's web joined the posts and blocked her way through. Because of its beauty, she could not break it off and by a round-about way managed to enter my garden. "What a lovely soul," I thought. "God will be glad that she did not destroy the diamond string. Such a soul as hers would be a true friend to Japanese poetry, because it is capable of appreciating reality, like that of the spider web changed to a diamond thread, when it assumes unexpected beauty.

Admitting the power of reality, is it more after all than a pound of sugar or butter? Like one who dislikes seeing Mount Fuji as a pile of lava, Japanese poets will keep a distance between themselves and reality. I know that the gesture of Intellect is ever tantalising and has a charm of a modern type, because of the evanescence in its movement; like a toe-dancer whose body is uncertain, Intellect leaves its feet on the ground. Where the individualist wishes to see the kaleidoscopic multiplicity of a thing, the Japanese poet abandons himself in the twilight of impersonality, to the Oneness that abides in Allness. Through Intellect one sees, for instance, the branches and leaves of a tree, and if he will, the structural process in them: while the poet sees the whole tree where the ghost of beauty lurks. Against the western theory that plays openly at vandalism, we sympathise with the angel of Beauty sobbing alone and in solitude.

We are glad to live in a forgotten castle of solitude where, unlike Rossetti's Helen melting the waxen knaves for her curse, we tell a rosary in self-respect because the silence watches us. Like the ordinary type of our race, not like the western poet who is of a race apart in his intellect or individuality, we Japanese poets are anxious to attain self perfection in the serenity of meditation. Steering away from the eloquence of poetry which makes us more hungry and restless, we gladly become men of few words, because we know enough of the invalidity of the human tongue. It may be said that, while we persist in dwelling on the beginning and the ending, the first and the last, western poets are busy talking about anything from the second to the ninth. If we are half-spoken, unintelligible, that is because, unlike western poets, we do not explain the midway at all. Take the following *Hokku* poem for instance:

Nanaye Yaye
  Hichido garan
Yaye Zakura.

(Seven-fold, eight-fold, —
  Seven-fold temple houses,
Eight-fold cherry-blossoms.)

What meaning can you draw from it, I wonder? The author of the poem, Basho, was at Nara in spring time, where he was impressed by the double-petalled cherry-blossoms, among which seven temple-houses were seen towering high,—that is the meaning of the poem. Whether you take it for childish babble in the beginning or for one's final conclusion, the ending depends on your choice.

I do not know whether this poem can be called a talisman as once a friend exclaimed in his enthusiasm for Japanese poetry. Tongue-tied in expression, no doubt it is, but it was enough to the author, because a poem was to him but a random note kept for himself, not a literary display which others should admire. Basho ably acquitted his qualification as a Japanese poet of few words.

Looking back upon the past literature of our country, we see with gratitude that, unlike western books which were mostly written for their readers, the popular diffusion of our books, at least in the past, was by accident and not by the fixed purpose of their authors. Till the middle seventeenth century when under the Tokugawa Shogunate with its popular art—Ukiyoye, the publication of books with a reading public in mind, fiction and miscellaneous works became prominent and produced professional writers and poets, most of the books still famous to-day were privately written for the enjoyment of the authors or for a few friends of their limited circles who shared their happiness. The Heian period (800-1200) is particularly distinguished in prose writing with lady writers like Murasaki Shikibu or Seishonagon, who, adorning the luxuriant and idle court of the time, reduced their brilliant and refined literature to the narrow compass of their own select society where they had their own literary solstice. As the name indicates and as Seishonagon has said somewhere in the work, Makura-no-Soshi, "Pillow Sketches," contains merely random notes jotted down to fill up leisurely moments: since there is no record of the process of its becoming popular, I can only say that, wherever a diamond is hidden, it will some day come to prominence. As the work was more or less a private memorandum, not a public display for readers to admire, the authoress may be excused for her language of frequent "innocent affectation and unconnected freakishness," because she had no reason to be fluent and intelligible to herself. Not only in the case of Seishonagon but for many others, particularly Hokku poets, whose work was but a spontaneous note of prayer spoken to their own lonely gods, you must assume the self-appointed office of making the original Imperfect perfect by your deliberation: hence, the difficulty of translating these works.

It is a matter of delight that by the eighth century Japanese literature had become already established as the utterance of a race-type, for in Manyoshu, "Collection of Myriad Leaves," the *Uta* poets whose vision was as clear as sunlight and as fresh as a plum blossom, awoke from sleep, and expressed themselves in statuesque idiosyncrasy. Those of a later date, however, are naturally flat in their work because of their structural advancement which sacrificed simplicity. We are glad that the then far-greater Chinese literature of the Soei and Tang dynasties which drifted into the country, did not cripple the heroic minds of the early poets, but only adjusted their shining vitality, as in the case of Hitomaru, to a better literary focus. If they transcend the lower region of criticism, that is because like poets of the morning, they exhausted spontaneously their inborn sensibility towards nature and life. However simple and crude they may be, their literary gravity is firm in racial aspiration. It is natural enough that, when we are tired and forget ourselves in multicoloured mental confusion to-day, we try to send back our minds to the Manyoshu age for a golden remedy. At an early age when, apart from the classics of the Greeks and Romans, no creditable book existed in Europe and literary sensibility was not yet developed there, we Japanese were already trying to find joy and sorrow in an amalgamation with nature, and kneeling before Eternity weaving life's beauty. We cannot help thanking our fore. fathers who, beginning their lives as lyrical adorers of nature, bequeathed us their sense of beauty which we have preserved with honour. If you doubt my words, you will see that even medieval records of clan-conflicts like "Genpei Seisuiki" or "Heike Monogatari," are not without the rich embellishment of poetical episodes in which fighters are really poets or musicians. But until western inıluence awoke the intellect of the present mind from hibernation, we Japanese had been only an emotional people who without pretending to criticise, adored nature and saw life only with a natural background. Yielding ourselves to the senses and to homely wits, we did not know how to rise from the literary lethargy in which we sought our self-satisfaction, when the harsh intellect of heterogeneous nature suddenly disturbed the peace of our fairyland seventy years age. The momentous question now is how we can establish our literary independence against the dazzling literature of the West. As I said before, we do not want to become a lost people in the world of literature, forgetting this adoration of nature a thousand years old, although we admit some changes in its expression and are glad for them.

At any rate western people will know that there is an island empire in the Far East where people for a thousand years have lived conforming to literary precepts and weaving a brocade with the warp and woof of nature and life. World history is busy recording the rise and fall of nations; the vicissitudes of a country's fortune cannot be different from that of a human life. Defying the law of mutability, Japan, one of the oldest countries of the world, still exists with a vitality which adapts itself to any situation. It is not a matter of self-satisfaction at all that we talk about the elixir which has kept us young. Again it is not from self-glorification that we spend many words on arts and literature to prove our past.

We admit that we Japanese are lacking in creative power, and do not aim, like western poets, at becoming rebuilders of life. We are taught not to deal with poetry as a mere art but to look upon it as the most necessary principle along which our real life shall be developed. When we kneel before poetry, it is our desire to create a clarified pure realm where we can arrange our minds. And then we recognize the existence of the compromising ground of passion, where we as members of society found our safety. The western poets were in the past earnest in their desire for the recreation of life, and not afraid when their desire reached its climax, even to risk reaching a condition of confused intricacy. I respect this western attitude in wishing to rebuild or recreate their own lives; and also I can well understand why they ascribe importance to their intellectual power. A great literary danger lies in this, of course, because there is nothing more sad and terrible for poets than to enslave themselves to intellect.

But we have also our own literary danger. I mean, that we often mistake a simple and cold morality for an art. I should like to know what is a more dangerous thing for poets than this sad morality. There are only few Japanese poets who have failed from their abuse of modes and passions; but we know so many cases wherein their poetical failure was quite complete under the stifling breath of conventional morality. This damage would not necessarily be below that inflicted by intellect;

it might be greater. We notice that the western poets often attempt to discover a poetical theory even in the waving plaits of Apollo's robe and analyse intellectually a little cloud flying in the sky. Admitting that their poetical theory and intellectual power are doubtless great, I have no hesitation in declaring it is they who harden, shrink and wither their own art. It is true to say that they owe much to the matter of form for the great development of their epics and dramas. Also it is true that the undeveloped form of Japanese poetry has given a mighty freedom for our poets to fly into an invisible spiritual domain. We can say again that, if these poets, both of the West and the East, often stray into the field of non-poetry, it is the result of their too close attachment to forms. Of course we must have more passion and intellect in our Japanese poets, and also properly tempered patience and effort. And at the same time we should hope that the western poets would forget their passion and intellect to advantage for entering into the real poetical life. We believe, not the moving dynamic aspect of all the phenomena, but their settled still aspect, that inspired the Japanese poets—at least the Japanese poets of olden days-to real poetry. But I know that the times are changing when we must, I think, cultivate the really living dynamic life. And I am afraid that such a new literary step may bring us into an unhappy compromise with western literature. Of course there are poets and writers both of East and West who know. only how. to compromise. But, on the other hand, we have a natural-born Westerner in the East, who will bring the East and West together into true understanding, not through faint-hearted compromise but by the real strength of independence which alone knows the meaning of harmony.

To-day we must read just the meanings of all things or give a new interpretation to all the old meanings: and we must solve the problem of life and of the world from our real obedience to laws and from knowledge that will make the inevitable turn to a living song, and learn the true meaning of time from the evanescence of psychical life; then our human lives will become true and living.

We must realise the ephemeral aspect of moments when time moves, and also the still aspect of infinity when it settles down; the meaning of moments out of the bosom of infinity; and again that of infinity from the changing heart of moments—that is the secret of real poetry. The moments that suggest the still aspect of infinity are accidental, therefore living; again the infinity that is nothing but another revelation of moments is absolute, therefore quiet and full of strength and truth. The real poetry should be accidental and also absolute. See the rivers and mountains and trees, see the smiling garden flowers, see the breaking clouds of the sky, see also the lonely moon walking a precipitate pathless way through the clouds. The natural phenomena are, under any circumstances, revealing both meanings of the accidentalism which is born from the absolute. When our great poets of Japan write only of a shiver of a tree or a flower, of a single isolated aspect of nature, that means that they are singing of Infinity from its accidental revelation. The poetical attitude of Wordsworth was anarchical when, singing of the small celandine, daisy, and daffodils, he gave even a little natural phenomenon a great sense of dignity by making it a centre of the universe, and broke the stupid sense of proportion by looking on things without discrimination; he was pantheistic, like nearly all Japanese poets and painters, because he was never troubled by any intellectual differentiation, and his clear and guiltless eyes went straight into the simplicity that joined the universe and himself into one. His poetical sensibility was very true and plain, and he gained a real sense of the depth of space, the amplitude of time, and the circle of the universal law, and made his life's exigency a new turn of rhythm. I am glad to think of Wordsworth as the first Easterner of English literature. If the Japanese poets teach the western poets anything, it is how to return to the most important feature of poetry after clearing away all the debris of literature; their expression is simple, therefore mysterious in many respects; as it is mysterious it is vivid and fresh. You must have a sense of adoration that comes only from poetical concentration. The followers of poetry in the imperishable raiment of silence sit before the inextinguishable lamp of adoration, by whose light they seek the road of emancipation. The house east of the forests, west of the hills, is dark without, luminous within, clothed with the symbols of the beauties of spirits and of heavens,—a wonderful place where the adoration has for a thousand years gone unchanged.

In this magical house of Faith the real echo of the oldest song will vibrate with the newest wonder, and even a simple little thought, once under the touch of imagination, grows more splendid than any art, more beautiful than life. It is never a question of the size of your song and your thought, but of adoration. We shall be at once brought back, if we are once admitted into this wonderful house, to the age of emotion and true love, where we speak only a few words of faith.

The Calcutta Review, July 1936

The Mask Play of Japan

Matsukaze, "The Pine-Wind," is one of the best specimens, rare and distinguished in Japanese *No* literature. It presents a nocturnal scene of Suma Strand where the fisherman's cry is ghostly under the shadow of the autumnal moonlight. Seeing this play which mingles beauty and sorrow, we respond as though to opium and are distressed by love in a reminiscent dream. And when towards the ending the two sad female ghosts, Pine-Wind and Shower, exclaim, "Alas, deluded still by dreams: Pray, speak a mass for our rest!" we manage to awake from ecstasy and sigh with relief. The chorus sings of a wind blowing in the back hills, and of the crows beginning to croak, and ends with the words: "There's none of the shower we heard? What remains there this morn is only the sound of the whispering pine." The characters of the play, three in all, withdraw behind the curtain. But in our imaginative ears the billow breaking at the strand is still faintly heard. The eastern sky becomes slowly bright.

As usual, a priest travelling "to see the beauties of various provinces" opens the play. He sees a roadside pinetree, the mark of the grave where the two fisher-maidens, Pine-Wind and Shower, are buried: he says: "Their memory is as fresh and green as the pine tree. Even the desolation of autumn is powerless against it." We have to imagine that evening twilight now encroaches on the scene of Suma Strand: beckoned by the magic wand of imagination, we should see that a sad lonely moon has already left the horizon. It is a night of preperception. Before us the two fisher-maidens appear at "*Hashigakari*," the long bridge-passage leading to the level of the stage; unlike people of their class, they wear brocade with silken overgarments of white. And they wear masks in which reality awakes to a world of imagery, a dream-world. Facing each other, they sing about the wagon (used to carry salt water which is made into salt) which they wheel tediously, turning towards the audience, on the Suma Strand where billows are restless and sad. "Alas, even the moon drenches her sleeves with tears," they cry in their song.

I always think that the success or failure of a play depends on the effects the actors inspire at this bridge, because in this introductory position they have a precious moment to hint the wonder of neutral emotion that waits to cry or smile at the touch of art. The bridge has no parallel in the world in form, and it responds in soft-white rhythm to their steps which never deviate from their centres of gravity, although they tremble with more than five senses. I find a perfect specimen of statuesque beauty in the two women, Pine-Wind and Shower, who are now entering the stage from the bridge. Saying that except the moon they have no friend in the world, they complain of their forlorn helpless lives, However, their sorrow, purified through poetical feeling, never departs from beauty. Their mental reserve is well suited to the scene!

The moon is lonely but bright in the sky, casting autumnal shadows on the tide that begins to flow. Approaching the strand to scoop up salt-water, they cannot help grieving over their miserable appearance that is reflected in the water. But recovering their spirits now, they resume their work. On the stage is placed one miniature wagon; on it two toy-like buckets. Now Pine-Wind opens her folding-fan, using it as a symbol of a dipper. With this fan-dipper she makes a gesture of scooping to the accompaniment of the chorus; again she gestures—putting the water into her buckets. She repeats the same gesture—there the buckets are half-filled, and then entirely filled,—and lo, the golden reflection of the moon is seen floating in the buckets. My friends, you must see them with your mind's eye. The art of the *No* play is that of the kingdom of imagination where the lack of anything is fruitful enough to bring forth something. Again it is the art of the kingdom of emptiness where, if you are a real dweller, you will know how to fill the emptiness with images where reality's pain and joy weave a brocade. This art of Japan is not one of falsehood, because it is the holy hall where one's soul, when it is true and poetical, walks in a passion-world of shadow to enjoy to the fullest its rarified sense and spirit. If you doubt my words, you should only see how like autumnal flowers drenched with moonlit dews, Pine-Wind and Shower loiter about ecstasy's perplexing by-roads; now they are seen carrying their wagon towards their hut near the strand,—you should imagine that they are doing so.

"Lo, my sister, the moon nestles in our buckets," Pine-Wind exclaims to Shower. Shower replies: "Yes, only one moon in the sky,—but we have two. Oh, how glad we are!" With the two moons in the wagon, their hearts smitten with life's distress now become lighter and they hurry home. Perhaps I might stop right here if my purpose were to tell only of the nocturnal beauty of the moonlit strand. When they arrive at their hut, they find the travelling priest waiting for them. They finally grant his request to stay there for one night, and say: "The moonlight tells that you are a renouncer of the world. If you don't mind the poverty of the hut, made of brushwood, with a pine-pillar and bamboo fence, you may come in." Received by the fisher-maidens, the priest sits by the fire to endure the cold night. He says that he spoke a mass before the grave of Pine-Wind and Shower when he passed by. And the priest is frightened to see the faces of the women changing with sudden tears. "We are no other than the ghosts of them," the women cry.

Interpreting the mind of Pine-Wind, the chorus speaks about Yukihira, a distinguished courtier and lover, who spent three years of love at the Suma Strand and, as a parting gift, left her his lacquered cap and garment. The prompter brings them out to the stage, and lets Pine-Wind hold them, who exclaims: "Alas and alack, what a remembrance, cruel yet sweet!" Pine-Wind holds up Yukihira's garment to her face and sobs and sobs. Standing up suddenly like a mad woman, approaching a miniature pinetree which is set on the stage as a property, Pine-Wind exclaims: "Oh, how glad I am to see My Lord standing there! Is it that my lordship is calling me? Yes, yes, I am coming, my lord!" Shower warns her that Yukihira is not there. Fixing her wild, maddened eyes on her sister, Pine-Wind exclaims: "How strangely you speak! How stupid! That pine tree is our lord certainly. Yukihira said that he should return if we 'pined,' though he parted from us. Now, did you forget his promise?" Shower recalls it and says weakly: "How irreverent I am not to remember his lordship's kind words! Indeed there he stands in the pinetree." She too becomes crazy. Then the two mad maidens run near the pinetree, calling it "Our sweet lord, our beloved!" Pinetree places Yukihira's garment on the pinetree. Both of them sob bitterly. The night advances. The moon is high in the sky and becomes brighter. The white sands and pebbles roar when the waves draw back. The winds blow.

Draw in your mind a sad picture of the two women possessed by love and delusion, who rave wildly under the lovely moonlight. Is there any theme more appealing than that? Love is a human feeling that is absolute and free. Its tremulous cadence brings an eternal note of sadness accentuated with beauty. Like a silken thread confused with neither beginning nor ending, the nocturnal world of phantasy presents itself in the "Pine-Wind." What a delicate yet powerful expression of life's rhythm rings in it! Any art which suggests the origin of humanity is worthy; we should feel in it some mysterious power that threatens and charms us alternately. The ecstatic world of feeling, where one is sad but not injured, stands on the borderland between reality and imagination; coiled round with mutual sympathy there, sadness and joy send forth their mist-like lustre, opaque yet beautiful. In this world nature and life are found symbolised, taking their self-enjoyment in the silence of abstraction at the last moment. However varied it be outwardly, the human feeling that flows there is simple and true. Within the shrine where Love is enthroned as their centre, all phenomena weave the soul's lamentation under faint moonlight creeping through the forest; and their song vibrates on the water of sentiment washing the sands of life's strand.

The nocturnal scene of the "Pine-Wind" is sad but sweet. Leaving finally with the words, "pray, speak a mass for our rest!" the two ghosts of love withdraw behind the curtain at the end of the long bridge where, in ghost-like fashion they cast their lonely shadows. The audience feels that they have sunk into the sea of eternity making no sound. The sea of eternity is calm. And this sea which swallowed up the two ghosts is undulating in heavy grey waves . . . . . . and it sleeps.

Yuya is a mistress of Munemori, a warrior of the Heike clan. She appears on the No stage wearing brocade and carrying a little fan, in her hand. Her mask has long slender eyes with the eyebrows high and wide apart, a ponderous, thick and flat nose, a mouth with white teeth and the underlip turning upwards. Not like that of the light and sagacious modern type, she smells of the soil. Where is there another mask like that of this Yuya with a face of emptiness which depends on one's whim of sensibility for interpretation? Reserving all passions, the mask gazes on a dream—a strange face indeed that cries under this smiling surface. Yuya is crying though in her heart, for she has received a missive from her mother now ill at home in the Yenshu province. The letter says in part: "There is neither flower nor moon that does not suffer eclipse. Even the Lord Buddha could not escape from the law of life and death, but passed away notwithstanding his promise to save the people of future ages. Lives of merely common order must be ready any day for death. So I am." Yuya's mother wishes her to return home before she dies. But her request for leave to go is denied by Munemori who orders the ox-cart to be drawn out, and bids Yuya to accompany him to a flower-viewing. Yuya is sad.

Now I would ask you if this masked woman still wears to you a face of emptiness. Is she not appealing to you now with all feelings that belong to a human being? And where is there another mask like this? Yuya is becoming even beautiful in spite of her flat nose. At any rate your imagination will permit me, I believe, to call her beautiful. The prompter brings a miniature cart with no ox, though the text says ox-cart, and it is an old-looking symbol. The characters, Munemori, Yuya and her maid Asagawo, are supposed to be in the cart, though they only stand beside it. You have to imagine that the cart is moving towards the Eastern Hill where the cherry blossoms are at their best; but the cart stands still on the stage. The chorus sings: "Among flowers there is one of eightfold petals and another single. If you unite them, you will have an ideal beauty of ninefold petals,—this famous city of ninefold glory has its own spring of springs." The time is spring day at the morning when the flowers exhaust their own beauty. The sky is hazy with the reflection of the natural display of the earth below.

Munemori's cart passes over the Bench of the Kamo River and stops at the Temple of Rokuhara Mitsuji where the Deity of Children is enthroned. Since she is reputed to save souls wandering and lonely, Yuya prays to the Deity begging her protection for her mother. She is sad. Passing now the crossway of the Six Roads by the Temple of Atago, the party comes to the Toriibe Hill where Yuya becomes still more sad at the sight of the curling smoke rising from a crematory. Her thought of the northern home is made more acute by a sudden bird in passage which flies towards the northern sky. Yuya is sad. Now she is arrived at Kiyomizu on the Eastern Hill; she leaves the cart at the temple gate and hurries towards the main hall where the Holy Goddess of Mercy has her throne. Yuya recites the pages of the sutra for her ill mother's sake.

Munemori prepares to have his flower-viewing feast here under the trees that are in full glory. Receiving her Lord's command, Yuya leaves the temple and reluctantly joins the party and even tries to look happy. But she is sad. "How beautifully the flowers bloom! Why don't you sing a song to make the feast lively?" Yuya is asked by his lordship. In spite of the sadness in her heart Yuya rises and sings:

The butterflies dance before the flower:
Lo, the snow falls and drifts!
The nightingales fly above the willow leaves:
Lo, gold threads fluttering in the wind!

Down by the running stream.
The odours come fast:
Separated by the wintry clouds,
The voice of a bell comes slow.

Yuya listens to the temple bell that carries to her a message of the transitoriness of things; she is sad. Gazing at the flowers blooming, she finds in their laughter the sad report of inevitable death. Interpreting Yuya's mind and gesture, the chorus dwells in song on the Temple of Keikyo and the Forest of Gion where the forest green is softened by the flower-clouds; then on this Kiyomizu Temple garden where the flowers are best. "Why do the winds sweep down the flowers so fast? Who knows how deeply Yuya suffers under the sad sight of falling petals!" Munemori asks her if she will entertain by dancing. Since she cannot but obey her lord, Yuya is sad. A shower falls while she dances. Turning her pale face to Munemori, Yuya says: "Alas, the shower makes the flowers fall, what do you think about it, my Lord?" Munemori replies to her murmuring: "What a heartless shower!" Yuya unfolds her fan, and raises it over her upturned forehead; then she gestures as if catching the falling petals with it. And she gestures lamenting over the passing spring. Yuya's tender mind thinks of the following old poem:

Are they tears or falling petals?
They are naught but the tears of spring rain.
Oh, who does not lament

The flowers falling down?

Prompted by this poem, Yuya gestures that she wishes to write her own poem,—this masked woman sorrowful of her mother lying low in her northern home. She folds her fan. Using it as a writing brush, she writes, no, pretends to write on a piece of paper which the prompter gives her. What Yuya writes is as follows:

The passing of spring in the capital
  Should be lamented,
But—oh, how the flowers of my northern home
  Fall and fall!

Munemori reads her poem. Moved with sympathy and regret, he exclaims: "I grant you leave now gladly. Depart, Yuya, as quickly as you desire!" "Oh, how glad I am, my lord," Yuya exclaims, and thanks the Goddess of Mercy by whose grace his lordship's coldness has been thawed. Yuya departs while the chorus sings that she turns toward the Eastern Highway where she finds a travelling companion in a bird who also hurries toward the northern sky. Is the play finished? No! We see Yuya still on the bridge-passage moving slowly towards the side-curtain,—she is still in the play, for the rhythm of the chorus still sings in our minds. Relieved of her fetters, thinking only of her mother, Yuya walks slowly but lightly, then disappears behind the curtain. We feel as though we are awaking from a dream, heavy but beautiful, where life takes on various colours of sentiment and mingles tears and beauty decoratively.

In Japan the spring, in spite of the beauty of its flowers is a season full of sadness and languor. It is spring that makes us think particularly of time's fast stepping feet. Even when we have no bad news as Yuya had, we cannot help feeling the melancholy undertone that spring plays. Therefore we say that spring wraps sadness with beauty. Where is there a Japanese who, when he sees Yuya, does not think of a cherry-blossom, sad yet beautiful, which will soon fall and perish?

My *No* play, if I ever write it, will take for its subject the story of Yang Kuei-fei. Being a beautiful woman whose "one glance would overthrow a city, two glances an empire," Yang was taken to the court of Ming Huang of the T'ang dynasty, and became his mistress. "Once she appeared," it is written "her beauty threw the thousand other women into the shade." The emperor grew at once infatuated with her, then became addicted to debauchery and even forgot to keep official audiences in the morning. This corrupt state of the court, revelling and feasting day and night, caused An Lu-shan's rebellion. Ming Huang fled from his gorgeous palace into the lonely province of Ssu-ch'uan but Yang met with tragedy for she was killed at the Ma-wai hill. Smitten with sorrow, the Sovereign commanded the Taoist of Lin Ch'ung to find Yang's lost soul by his wizardry. Obeying the august decree, the religious magician went down to the Eternal Spring below, and then over the thousand waves of the sea to the Isle of the Blest only to be discouraged in his efforts. Now as a final attempt, the Taoist decided to get up to Heaven, the Empyrean above. My play begins here. I will make the chorus sing how the Taoist flies from cloud to cloud, and how he swims from star to star. "How glad I am," the Taoist exclaims, when he has almost finished the bridge-passage with his fast steps, "to be near the city of Eternity! Behold the palace rising like a rain-bow! What splendour!—surpassing that of the sovereign's Hibiscus Hall where dance and laughter frightens away the dullness of the night!" Of course not even a toy house is brought on the stage for an indication of the palace; the listeners' imagination must respond to the chorus. The Taoist finds the jade western gate, and loiters about there, wishing to know who is enthroned as queen.

Ordinarily *No* play characters appear and exit through the bridge, but I will make Yang sit from the beginning on the left side of the stage near the chorus; she is now supposed to be in the palace, standing by a window near the western gate where the Taoist loiters. She says that she has now returned home from the lower world, where, among the flames of love and wine, she passed her temporary life in the Sovereign's sweet favour, but she cannot forget, she says, how suddenly the song of the Rainbow Skirt and Feather Jacket was stopped by the roll of the rebel war-drum. "Oh, how painful it is to recollect my flight," she exclaims, "Oh, what a sad memory that is! At this moment a singing voice is heard from behind the stage as if from a distance:

> The dust clouds rise by the ninefold city;
> A thousand horses and chariots to the south-west
> move.
> Feathers and jewels onward and then a halt:
> A hundred miles from the city on the west,
> The soldiers refuse to advance, nothing can be done
> with them;
> Alas, in sight of them the moth-eyebrowed beauty
> is forced to die.
> On the ground lie ornaments with nobody to pick
> them up,
> Kingfishers' wings, golden sparrows, and hairpins
> of jade.
> The sovereign covers his face, powerless to save;
> Turning back, he lets flow his tears and blood.

The Taoist speaks aloud saying that he is an ambassador sent by the emperor, asking if the queen of the palace is within. "I desire to speak to her," he exclaims. Responsive to the voice, Yang pushes away the flower-like curtains, and descends from the jewelled turret. She is beautiful. Lo, her face powdered and painted, with cloud-like hair!

Like a spray of peach blossoms on a rain-wet spring morn, Yang's beauty is now subdued, and she asks the ambassador what message he has brought her. The Taoist says that on account of her death Ming Huang's heart is never brightened by the brightness of the moon, and the sound of a bell mingled with the evening rain only gives him painful memories. "The Ssu-ch'uan hills and the Ssu-ch'uan water are ever dark," the Taoist exclaims, "for the Sovereign is consumed by grief and tears." Again the sound of singing is heard from the distance:

In the hibiscus he sees her face, in the willow her eye-brows;
How should not his longing tears flow.
When the peach or plum blooms in spring breezes,
When in autumn rain the wu-t'ung leaves fall?
To the south of the western palace are many trees,
But the fallen leaves on the steps no one sweeps.
The Pear-Garden entertainer's hair is white as if with age,
The beauties of the Pepper-Chamber look no longer young.
The fireflies flit by the even hall only to make him sad;
Even when the lone lamp is burnt out, he still fails to sleep:
The slowly passing watchers tell that the night is long;
Clearly shine the constellations as if the morn would never come.
The kingfisher coverlet is cold with none to share its warmth:
Parted by life and death, time still goes on;
Never once does her spirit come back even in his dream.

The Taoist approaches her; looking into her face, he says how glad he is to find her as beautiful and young as of old. Then he assures her that he has been sent by the Sovereign to render her in person his words of longing. Yang replies to the Taoist, saying: "How since we parted I have missed his form and voice! Our love on earth came so soon to an end, but days and months in the Empyrean are long, so in longing I suffer the more. Oh, how often I turn and gaze down towards the world and mortal life! Oh, how I cry because I do not see the Sovereign's City in mists!"

The Taoist says that the Sovereign would be glad to know his ambassador had met her and received her words of love. "But I pray," the movement, the chorus sings: "Taking out one half of her jewelled gold hairpin, the Lady Yang says: "Tell the Sovereign to keep this till here in heaven or in the earth below we two meet again—till we meet again!"

But the Taoist doubts the Sovereign will believe him, because such a thing as hairpin is common in the lower world; he wishes to give some more particular thing that the Sovereign recognizes as belonging to her alone. Yang recalls how on the seventh day of the seventh moon, in the Hibiscus Hall where no one was near, the Sovereign whispered in her ear, after pledging two stars in the sky: "In heaven we will ever fly like one-winged birds, on earth, grow joined like trees with branches inter-twined." (Each bird must fly with a mate, since it has only one wing.) There would be nothing, Yang thinks, better than those words to prove that the Taoist had seen her, since they are words only the Sovereign and herself know. Then through the chorus Yang says that, since her worldly body was lost at the Ma-wai hill, the promise about one-winged birds and branch-twined trees had become meaningless. "But my changeless soul," she exclaims, "still longs for the day when we shall meet again."

The Taoist is now glad that he can return to the Sovereign's side with success; he is sad, however, that he cannot take her with him to the world. When he bids farewell, Yang wishes to tarry yet for a while for she will dance him the dance of the Rainbow Skirt and Feather Jacket to make their parting a little happier. Yang dances dwelling on past days when song and dance in unison with guitar and flute made the Sovereign's harem an endless revel, night and tears unknown. While dancing, Yang cries. The chorus sings: "Who will know the Lady Yang's heart? Alas! she cries! Her tears descend to the lower world and to the peach trees at the beginning of the spring. Lo, snow-white dews on the blossoms! Read among their petals the sad story of the beautiful Yang Kuei-fei!" Then the singing voice is heard dying away in the far distance:

> Heaven lasting, Earth long, will some day pass
> away;
> But her sorrow shall be forever, forever and aye!
> Heaven lasting, Earth long, will some day pass
> away;
> But her sorrow shall be forever, forever and aye!

Among three hundred pieces now in existence, there is none, perhaps, like "The Robe of Feathers" that so gracefully portrays the delicate, statuesque beauty of composition and sentiment. It is a play about a fairy whose feather-robe was stolen by a fisherman at Mio's pine-clad shore, while she was bathing, and upon her promise to dance, was evidently given back. Not to go to extremes, even in sadness, is taught in Japan to be the height of cultured manners; here we have every Japanese beauty and lamentation embodied in this fairy, who could not fly back to the sky, and sang:

> Vainly my glance doth seek the heavenly plain,
> Where rising vapours all the air enshroud,
> And veil the well-known paths from cloud to cloud.

And she promised that she would dance the dance that makes the Palace of the Moon turn round, and would leave her dance behind as a token to mortal men, if her robe could be restored her. However, the fisherman doubted whether she might hurry home to heaven without dancing at all, then the fairy said:

> Fie on thee! The pledge of mortals may be doubted,
> but in heavenly beings there is no falsehood.

Since the plays are the creation of the age when, by virtue of Sutra or the Buddha's holy name, any straying ghosts or spirits in Hades were enabled to enter Nirvana, it is no wonder that most of the plays deal with those ghosts of Buddhism. That ghostliness appeals to the poetical thought even in the modern age, because it has no age. It is the essence of Buddhistic belief, however fantastic, to remain poetical forever.

Although the repertory does not change, our conception and understanding will be altered; it is the reason why the *No* plays can always keep fresh themselves. We have one play called "Yama Uba," or "Mountain Elf," reminding us that we are souls, troubled in a maze of transmigration. Like the Mountain Elf, we should be spending all the dark night in wandering round the mountain. That mountain is a symbol of life itself. The story is about a famous dancer called Hyakuma Yama Uba, a woman who has earned a reputation for her portrayal of the Mountain Elf circling round the mountain. She has lost her way in Agero no Yama in a pilgrimage toward Zenkoji, the Holy Buddhist Temple; and here she meets the real Elf or Yama Uba, with large star-like eyes and fearful snow-white hair, who demonstrates to her how she encircles the mountains, nay the mountain of life. The play ends as may be expected: the Elf, the nocturnal dancer round the mountains, at last disappears, as her life's cloud of perplexity is cleared away, and the dust of transmigration is swept aside. This little play would certainly make a splendid subject for modern interpretation. When "Yamauba" has been on the stage, I have seldom missed seeing it for the nocturnal scene which the chorus introduces to our imaginative eye, the moaning voice of pine trees echoing far down to a trembling valley-water, where the ghostly demoness looms up. How she stretches her gruesome body towards the "mountain rising but from a speck of dust and thrusting itself into the clouds," how she bends herself over the boundless sea with the moon nestling in its heart.

No doubt you will be moved now to smile and now to cry

with the actors wearing the same mask of painted wood, which, marvellously enough, seems capable of differentiating the most delicate shades of human feeling. We should thank our own imaginations which turn the wood to a spirit more alive than ourselves, when neither the actors nor the mask-carvers can satisfactorily express their secret. We know that the mask is made to reserve the feelings, and that the actors protect themselves wonderfully well from falling into the bathos of so-called realism through the virtue of poetry; but when we realize it is from the same old humanity that tears and smiles arise, and brothers or sisters of actual blood relationship spring forth, their difference being only a little shade of colour, the mystery that the *No* hall performs on our human minds will be explained to a very great measure. This is the house of imagination, where those who can only find strength from the crudity of their five senses have no right to enter, but where the silent worshippers of the Imperfect will congregate for the holy exercise of the ritual of their imaginations. It is not the whole truth to say that it is the *No*'s dignity that commands one to believe in its representation, though one may incline to think otherwise, as, for instance, in the case where the character of a lady, whose voice and posture are not different from a man's, is represented on the stage; but it is for the poetical mind to object to seeing the superficial reality, and to surrender all criticisms for the sake of appreciation. The actual expression of the *No* stage is extremely slight and ephemeral, like many other expressions, such as the sighs of crickets or the trembling of flowers. We gain, as we behold it, great courage at an almost astonishingly low cost of human energy. It goes without saying that the plays themselves are brief; and one has many reasons to be thankful that the stage has never from its beginning to the present day been troubled with the dropping curtain, because the curtain only serves to bar the stage, to remind us always that we have to restrain ourselves and not come into too close communication with the actors. And what use is the *No* hall if one cannot drop the curtain in one's imagination? I have had occasion before to associate the *No* hall with the tea-room, where, through the fragrance of tea, the melody of the boiling kettle and the curl of incense, one will surely enter the twilight land of the unknowable. When we are told that both of them were practically formed, encouraged and developed under the rule of the Ashikaga lords of the 14th century, who attempted and even succeeded in their attempt, to invigorate human lives with that lesson of simplicity, the comparison will not seem a mere spiritual speculation.

And was there ever a time like to-day when the complex is replacing the homogeneous, when we need such a lesson in all the aspects of life? What variety and richness have we earned from making the entire sacrifice of that simplicity? We should remember that the simplicity and archaism of the so-called tea-ceremony grew out of the purism of the Zen monastery, or priest hall of meditation. It will be seen that the dominant desire was after the ideal of beauty.

We are happy to see the *No* plays on the stage, the actors succeeding beautifully in developing poetical yearning. It is their best art that they make the expression of humanity, if there is any humanity in the plays, gracefully subordinate to poetical harmony. The lines which the actors sing or, more properly, recite loudly, with the alternation of the chorus, of course take the main part in creating the beautiful effect of the scene. Under their passionate intensity the characters rhythmically break the statuesque stillness of their surroundings. Although the actors express flexible delicacy to its utmost degree, one cannot help observing, on the other hand, some strange pervading power which makes one feel overwhelmed, uncomfortable, scarcely able to breathe. This might be from the too serious nature of the plans which always demand the most honest and cautious interpretation, and make the actors too afraid of destroying their effect or atmosphere.

It is seldom, when they are good, that the actors destroy the general harmony of the plays by giving way to the temptation to expose themselves and their own personalities beneath the masks they are wearing. Their acting can be compared with an old brocade, rich and luxurious. And one will be surprised to discover what a dynamic power they have. No other form of drama has so close a connection with Buddhism; in fact, there is not a single play in which does not appear a priest whose divine power of meditation or prayer invariably leads the ghost of a warrior or a lady, a flower or a tree into the blessing of Nirvana. To call the *No* the ghost play has no real meaning, any more than to call it the priest play. Their main point is to express the human tragedy rather than the comedy of the old stories and legends as seen through the Buddhistic understanding, for most of the plays, were written by people who were strongly influenced by the holy faith. They were fermented under the encouragement of the Ashikaga lords from the fourteenth century down to the close of the sixteenth century. It was in those days, that in the History of Japanese literature the various traditions and legends, the certain Buddhistic faith and imagination hitherto neglected by the aristocratic literature of the Kyoto court were first dressed in pure literature. Yoshimitsu, the third lord of the Ashikaga government, the propagandist of the tea ceremonies and refined arts may be said to have been the first encourager; and at the time of Yoshimasa, the eighth lord, the plays as we have them to-day had been roughly completed. In due time, Ashikaga's power declined; and the most wonderful war god arose on the horizon in the person of Hideyoshi, the Napoleon of Japan, who, on the other hand, was a patron of art and literature. The plays were not left in oblivion in his time, but many new pieces were added to the already great repertoire, and alterations were made in those already in practice. When the Tokugawa feudal era of the seventeenth century, the period of peace and prosperity, arrived, the play had become the most important factor in the nation's life. To recite lines from them, and to act them on the stage, if possible, were regarded as a gentleman's accomplishments; in contrast with the common plays they were the most dignified, noble form of entertainment. And so it is to-day.

Let me say again that the aim of the *No* play is to express a desire or yearning, not for beauty, but for the beauty we dream; therefore the value of the play depends, not upon the truth or humanity treated, but upon the total effect of the beauty produced, which is poetry freed from any obligation toward reason or fact. Edgar Allan Poe's poetical principles are not alien to this idea: he says, "We struggle by multiform combinations among the things and thoughts of time to attain a portion of that loveliness whose very elements, perhaps, appertain to eternity alone." The purpose of these combinations and rearrangements in the case of the *No* play is, of course, to make the expression of eternal order more distinct and beautiful. And the *No* play, simply by virtue of being emotional, is pleased to understand this eternal order not as truth or morality, but as beauty, which includes everything. The elements of stories in the plays are valuable only because they are the means of approach to the final great end, which is to excite or elevate the soul by the demonstration of eternal order. In fact, the stories themselves are secondary matters.

It is seldom that a *No* play forgets the poetical effect which is its first and last concern to create. It is clear that the actors must protect themselves from falling into the bathos of reality which would alienate, them from the rhythmical creation of beauty. Again Poe says: "And in regard to truth—if, to be sure, through the attainment of a truth we are led to perceive a harmony where none was apparent before, we experience at once the true poetical effect: but this effect is referable to the harmony alone, and not in the least degree to the truth which merely served to render the harmony manifest." In such language Poe might have spoken of the *No* plays, which, at their best, have not only to reveal their art, but also to conceal it.

Some well-known actors, as, for instance, Mr. Manzaburo Umewaka or Roppeida Kita, are rich in a remarkable voice, remarkable at any time and in any place, which might make us recall an old phrase, "the rolling jewels upon a glass board." Their command over their large, round, deeply vibrating voices is both spontaneous and well calculated. Their vocal training, that begins in their boyhood days, is founded on their energetic and sensitive emotion of life. To hear them on the stage, at least to us Japanese, is a treat at such a time as the present, when actors of any school are but little more than human phonographs.

Some critic writes on the way actors treat verse as a slightly more stilted kind of prose: "When they come to a passage of purely lyric quality they give it as if it were a quotation, having nothing to do with the rest of the speech." In all the rendering of the lines of *No* plays, the actors are taught not to forget they are at the same time the direct expression of the characters and of poetry, that is, a thing with its own reasons for existence. They might give, I think, many a suggestion to the poets of the West, who are eager to invent some vocal manner between speaking and singing. Strictly speaking, the rendering of the words of a *No* play should be called speaking, not singing; therefore there is the danger of over-emphasizing the meaning. But when the actors fall sometimes into the danger of overemphasizing the sound, it is then that their natural wealth of vocalism runs wild and becomes careless. It goes without saying that they are superb when their gift is well regulated.

The Calcutta Review, September 1936

Kinchinjanga

It dawned at Siliguri three hundred and fifty miles to the south of Calcutta. In one night I spent in the train the season changed from autumn to winter.

All the travelling outfits fastened at the back of a motor car. I was now ready to run up a mountain road for fifty miles towards Darjeeling. The plain soon lost itself in a heavily-shadowed forest. Leaving bamboo bushes and mangoes behind, I found that Nature began to feast me with kaleidoscopic changes when the road became steep and zigzag. Looking down the ravine and seeing hundreds of red flowers among the ferns crowded like clouds, I could not help thanking Nature, whose feminine heart kept her own kindly tenderness even at a lonely spot forgotten by humanity. I leave to your imagination how unsettled I felt because, even before I reached Sookna in the distance of seven miles from Siliguri, my motor-car made turning a hundred times, and that almost in mad reeling pace.

Kurseong, a town five thousand feet above sea-level, greeted me with a huge sunflower that would not fail to please anybody, a Wilde or a Blake. Among the beggars around me there was an old Tibetan who, like the Buddhist that he looked, wore a rosary on his neck and muttered something mysterious. I amused for a moment staring at his outlandish face linked with a Japanese No-mask of Ebisu, an ebony black nondescript god of wealth, whose original home was a subject of frequent discussion among the archaeologists. And when I saw another interesting specimen in a human peacock, the Tibetan widow whose ear-lobes were decorated with large pieces of gold, I wondered that female freak of an idle rich was not a tantalising problem restricted in New York or London.

The fog grew deeper with the progress of the motor-car, now drawing near Darjeeling; the zigzag road increasing its bends looked so narrow under the gloomy dusk that forbade me to see ten feet ahead. I thanked, however, my driver, whose adroit handling of the car relieved my mind of a foolish fear of nose-dive into a bottomless ravine. Through the fog a few strange human shadows approached when my car stopped to make them pass by. Finding them to be but French missionaries of the Roman Church who lived with God in a lonely mountain in this neighbourhood, I could not help admiring of their religious heroism. I thought, with gratitude, that the spiritual kingdom was not wholly lost in the world.

When I arrived at Darjeeling, the young clerk of Everest Hotel welcomed me in Japanese and said: "You are a Japanese poet, I believe; we had been following your movement since you arrived in Calcutta. How we looked forward to your coming here!" Since I did not come for the Japanese words to such a distant place near the Tibetan frontier, I looked at him with amazement and doubt. Being told that he mastered our language during two years he spent in Yokohama. I felt all the more decidedly the smallness of the world. I asked him, when I was shown to my room, whether I could expect good weather for tomorrow; he replied: "No one would be responsible for weather. But it will clear off tonight—at least, I hope so."

Leaving weather to God's whim, I left my room and went out for seeing a bazaar where I soon added a Japanese to a dirty but picturesque exhibition of swarthy races, Lepchas, Limbus, Bhatias, Nepales, Paharias, Tibetans, Bengalies and Kasmiris. They smelled pretty bad. There were many booths or sheds where bird feathers, red or green, a fur with black spots and rugs hemmed round with painted elephants linked together were shown for sale; I found also there hundreds of brass plates and bottles, decorated with strange tropical flowers, inlaid sparsely with beads in blue or vermilion. And on the rush-mat of a street-stall fried beans, pickled vegetables, salted fishes and other tit-bits were on sale beside cheap perfumes, printed cottons and flannels.

I returned to my hotel room when the fog suddenly cleared off, and through the window pane Kinchinjanga, a jumbled mass of diamonds, was seen in the distance half-buried in the foaming sea of clouds. The mountain sanctified in thin air, was too sublime to look at, being absolutely unapproachable for us human beings; it was a natural citadel shown by God who put our wonder or fear to the test. Fancying that there in the mountain should be living some people far more noble than ourselves, I retired to my bed for a little rest to free myself from fatigue. But after a little while I woke up from sleep, and to my surprise I found God to be a capricious artist who rubbed away Kichinjanga from his canvas with the fog.

I left my bed before three o'clock in the next morning, cheered up by a cleared sky, studded all over with brilliant stars. I finished simple breakfast, a toast and cup of tea, anticipating a wonderful sunrise to be seen at Tiger Hill six miles away. When all prepared with mid-winter clothes I stood before the hotel entrance, six Tibetan coolies were ready with an open vehicle, Jinrikisha, as we called it in Japan, the long handles of which were soon lifted by them. Turning to right and left, the winding road gradually grew steep and dark when town lights were left behind. Unknown to the location, I felt as if carried off through a dismal cavern walled by the bushes and trees that rustlingly replied to my vehicle in panting progress. This ghostliness was more intensified when the coolies began to sing in Tibetan, whether to inspirit themselves or to amuse me or to frighten a beast awaiting to assault. When their songs in a weird and hoarse voice stopped, the hoofs of a horse, on which my Indian servant rode, were heard ringing up to the stars.

Raising my face from among the blankets, I noticed that, daybreak drawing near, the stars already had lost their former brilliancy and the sky now became slightly pale. Through a faint light that resembled mists, I saw the jumbly tree and bushes to right and left, where a few early risers of birds already chirped in greeting a zealous climber. Before I reached the top of Tiger Hill my servant ran up whipping his horse because he had to build there a fire for my warming. It was so cold that my body stiffened, but air that kissed my cheeks was fresh and fragrant with promise of a splendid dawn. The fire my servant prepared was brightly burning on the top of the hill where I soon stood. Not drawing near the fire, I held my head high against the wild sea of clouds that almost rose from my feet; but I trembled in the face of Kinchinjanga, a triangled array of diamonds, rising above that cloud-sea as a divine agency.

Receiving the first benediction of the sun when others were not yet relieved of the night, the mountain commanded, as I perceived it, the world to be ready for welcoming the dawn. The new moon in the low eastern sky, an Indian lady's eyebrow, now vanished into obscurity because, after a fashion becoming to tender heart, she was afraid to be seen by the sun. Silence that ruled the world still quite dark was profound. But the silence began to break when the red fringe of the sun appeared from beyond the horizon. One minute passed, two minutes passed, three minutes passed when the sun, now a round fan of vermilion, floated up making the sea of clouds a sea of seething blood. Oh, how Kinchinjanga sparkled in gold! What a sight; what grandeur!

My Indian servant who stood by me suddenly exclaimed: "look, look; look at Everest!" Turning my head towards the way he pointed, I saw Mount Everest silently saluting a Japanese visitor from afar. But in a few minutes, alas, the divine ghost disappeared.

I have now seen the view which was permitted only for a few. Thinking it too holy for one's long admiration, mistrusting, too, God who might play the wilful artist again to wipe the scene away, I made preparation to descend the hill.

The Spectator, August 1936

Indian Impressions

I happened to be in Nagpur towards the end of December last year, and to see there something of the "Golden Jubilee of the Indian Congress," a quite exciting national affair, naturally not devoid of self-glorification. Accompanied by Justice Niyogi, I left Maharaj Bagh Garden where a reception and speeches were given, and then visited a Swadeshi exhibition a short distance away. The electric lights shone brightly over the booths heavily loaded with a hundred industrial products, clay toys from Lucknow and Madras, brass plates and rugs from Kashmir, and all sorts of homespun cotton cloths. The first thing I saw there was a large picture suspended high in the air by ropes, in which Gandhi, a smiling toiler at the spinning wheel, was seen clothing a lady, the central figure of the picture. The purpose of this pictorial advertisement, the propagation of the domestic cotton industry, was emphasized, as I soon found when going round the exhibition, by five or six women who were demonstrating their spinning art on a small wooden machine.

The Indian hand spinning-wheel, Charkha as it is called, is a simple but precise machine, something like the one we used to see in our Japanese villages half a century ago. The cheapest Charkha, I am told, does not cost more than three rupees. I do not know when Gandhi began to propagate the use of this machine, but the amount of cotton cloth which village people of India produce by their own hands today, I understand, is as much as three hundred thousand yards. This subsidiary industry has already proved to be a vital factor in Indian village life and it is not too much to say that, if Gandhi's Charkha movement becomes more generalized throughout the country, the solution of the problem of subsistence, at least in part, through "self-support and self-sufficiency," will not be far distant. Doubtless, this homespun cotton cloth, a specimen of which I had seen in the dress of Pandit Malaviya of the University, Benares, has no refinement like that of the cloths which modern factories produce with scientific uniformity, but beauty is perceptible beneath its rustic homeliness. Considering the real conditions of the country, where development of the highly organized modem factories would bring ninety-nine people out of one hundred to starvation for one man's benefit, and where the vast plains, lean and waste, cannot easily be made productive, there is nothing more momentous for India today than the lesson of "self-support and self-sufficiency."

It is foolish to sell a product cheaply as raw material, only buying it back again at a high price when it assumes a different appearance. The history of the spinning-wheel in India, it is said, is as old as the Vedas. And the people have inherited a legacy of skill in handling it. The rigours of the climate drive them within doors during half the year. If they are busy turning the wheel there, their minds are troubled by neither religion differences nor hatred hatched from the caste system, and they can save themselves from evil thoughts that enslave them in idleness. Since they are not labourers depending on other, they are not in danger of being thrown out of employment. They can sell their production any time when it is more than they need for their homes. I agree with the believers in the Charkha, Gandhi's followers, who say that, apart from material considerations, the spiritual effect of the wheel is of the utmost significance because its buzzing sound causes people to forget life's ills.

Leaving Nagpur for Bombay, I stopped over at Walda, an insignificant country town but the spiritual centre of the Gandhi movement. I was glad to see Gandhi with a fitting background in his Ashram, a monastery or refuge, where, unlike the ardent ascetic, this modern prophet responds to every pulsation of hope or pain in his nation's life. In view of his illness, he was lying down in a tent pitched upon the flat roof of a two-storeyed concrete house, square in form with a yard in the centre. I found him with a saintly little smile revealing his broken teeth, stretching out his bare legs, as lean as a cricket's and as stiff as steel wire, which one of his disciples was shampooing. I found difficulty in connecting this seemingly simple and unaffected man with the heroic fasts that had made the mammoth soul of England once tremble in fear. Noticing that he put on his head something wrapped in cotton cloth, I asked him what it was. He said that it was wet earth which, according to his doctor's advice, was good for a man like him whose blood pressure was high. Then with a smile in which cynicism and philosophy commingled, he exclaimed: "I sprang from Indian earth. So it is Indian earth that crowns me."

After a little talk, I bade him farewell and descended the stairs to meet three or four of his disciples, who were waiting to take me round the Ashram. Passing by a place containing beehives, I was taken into a shed to see a bull turning a stone mortar and making oil out of rape-seeds. Then I went to another place where paper-making experiments were in progress. One of the disciples said: "How simple it is to make paper! If this paper-making becomes popular in our country as a subsidiary industry, we shall be able to keep a great deal of money at home." It need hardly be said that the spinning-wheel, the Charkha, holds an important position in the Ashram. A little flat wooden box was brought out, which revealed, when uncovered, a miniature wheel invented by Gandhi himself during his leisure moments in prison. The explainer said: "You can put it even into a hand-bag and carry it in the train to fill the vacant hours by turning it."

Then he said further: "Gandhi is remarkably scientific. And his patience always brings his inventive mind to complete success. Had he been a watch-maker, he would have the best watch in the world to his credit. As a surgeon or a lawyer, he would also fill the highest place. But describing himself as a farmer and a weaver by profession at his trial in 1922, he pledged himself to the sacredness of manual labour. Among the various kinds of such work he regards weaving most highly, because it gives one a habit of exactitude and a mental training in keeping strictly to the law of economy. Gandhi hates waste more than anything else. Believing that manual labour alone can give a new life to India, he makes the Charkha his own symbol, and calls the people to the holy banner of an independent life." It is only incidental that his movement appears to be a rebellion against the British yoke, because, while seeking to save India from corruption, it would also save the other countries of the world through its great lesson of creative energy, the propagation of life close to the soil. The importance of service within one's immediate surroundings as against a groping after distant ideals is not limited to India only; the manliness of the "self-supporting and self-sufficing" Swadeshi spirit must be recognized through all time and throughout the whole world.

Gandhi cannot find any higher way of worshipping God than by serving the poor and identifying himself with them. When he goes on a railway journey, for instance, he always takes a third-class ticket reminding himself that he also belongs to the lower orders of mankind where humanity and love are found to be the richest. As one who has spent the best part of his life with working-class people and has shared joys and sorrows with them equally, Gandhi offers to his friends the spinning wheel as an inspiration of the "self-supporting and self-sufficing" life.

I left Gandhi's house when the sun was still high in the sky, but afternoon breezes already began to kiss one's cheeks. Like the other Indian towns, Walda was half buried in feathery sands and dust, which cows and sheep shared with loin-clothed men, saints or loafers. Passing through the streets, I was delighted with the glorious oranges which made a street-stall of rush-mats look so beautiful. At the station a large basket containing a hundred fruits from Gandhi's orchard had been sent with his compliments to await my arrival.

Lying alone in my compartment of the train for Bombay, I could not put away from my mind for some time the image of Mahatma Gandhi. Once I had the pleasure of reading his little essay entitled "Voluntary Poverty," in which he expressed his joy at discarding the things that belonged to him before. He says: "One after another the things slipped away from me. And I can say a great burden fell off my shoulders, and I felt that I could now walk with ease and do my work likewise in the service of my fellowmen with great comfort and still greater joy." For anybody in a country like India to live with anything more thin bare necessities, he believes, means living like a robber. Unless you be like one who sleeps outside with nothing on his body, you have no right to declare that you can save India and the Indians. I am told that even the cloth with which Gandhi covers his loins is reduced to the very minimum. He loves Daridranaryana, "God of the Poor," because, to use his own words, "he is the most sacred, inasmuch as he represents the untold millions of poor people as distinguished from the few rich people." It was natural that Gandhi should advance from this eulogy of poverty into asceticism through which one's five senses are to be controlled as a method of self-purification. Therefore, the fasting with which he astonished and frightened the world some years ago was to him nothing extraordinary at all.

Through his periodical, *Harijan*, meaning "Untouchable," Gandhi is now striving with all his might for the emancipation of this unfortunate class; identifying himself with its interests, I understand, he adopted one of its people as his son. There is no greater barrier to India's unification than the caste system. Until this unreasonable convention breaks down, the establishment of a strong nation with each person as a unit on an equal footing cannot be realized. I know of no other country where love and mercy are talked about so eloquently as in India. Yet, since the day of Buddha so many great Indians, saints and reformers, have left their talk on humanity in their books. It is appalling even to think what a great task lies before Gandhi and his followers. Gandhi sought to bring love into politics with his doctrine of "Non-violence," and in doing so he did not address himself alone to the British people. His spiritual power was so great that he forced the whole world to face the question of whether or not it was irrevocably lost to love. Yet, it was true that he brought actual struggle nearer, while the heaven he created was only that of spiritual triumph. Now, leaving politics to others, he enters into a larger kingdom where he associates himself with eternity. He will feel safer, I am sure, like Browning's "Patriot," to be paid by God what the world owes him.

I visited Sarnath near Benares, one of Buddha's landmarks in India, where a handful of Buddhist priests, in keeping with the atmosphere of the lonely ruins, were lighting candles to the "Holy Wheel of the Law." Between self-mortification and austerity on the one hand, and indulgence and pleasure-seeking on the other, Buddha found a "Middle path," the doctrine on which he based his "Eight Tenets of Righteousness." Seeing how Indian minds swing from asceticism to worldliness, from one extreme to the other, Buddha's doctrines, I think, should be accepted even today as a living light. And the human suffering from disease and poverty, which caused Buddha to leave his happy castle in a search for religious truth, exists today almost unchanged. I have no mind to ascribe Gandhi's initiation of his relief movement to the same spectacle, and I do not know why I should connect him with Buddha, but Gandhi and Buddha both agree in love and "Non-violence." And both of them sought light in prayer; to them prayer was never a refuge of cowardice, but the spiritual stronghold where the soul's perfection should be protected. In a little essay, "Prayer," Gandhi says: "Prayer has not been a part of my life as truth has been. Prayer came out of sheer necessity. I found myself in a plight where I could not possibly be happy without prayer. The more my faith in God increased, the more irresistible became the yearning for prayer. Life seemed to be dull and vacant without it." While Buddha preached of Nirvana, Gandhi surrendered to his immediate surroundings, attempting to solve the problem of human need through his spinning wheel. I surely believe that for Gandhi this simple machine buzzes as a prayer to God, as does the Buddhist prayer-wheel.

On one of a few occasions when, leaving poetry and art, I talked of politics and social reform, Yajineswara Chintamani, a journalist in Allahabad, assured me that politically India today is standing still. That was what I expected, since England seemed disposed to leave the Indians to indulge in their passion for perpetual talk. Besides, the sense of justice, no doubt a great moral asset among individuals, is hardly powerful enough to break the net-work of international politics. Coming to immediate questions, Chintamani dwelt on the farm-village life, saying that without knowledge of it one would be unqualified fully to understand India's agony. He said: "How appalling it is to see starving farmers only too glad to have the washed rice water from their rich neighbours!" Although I had no time to make a study of rural conditions, I was given several opportunities during my journey of five thousand miles in India to have glimpses of the poor village life. Covering their waists with a dirty rug, women were seen by a falling mud house, the inner darkness of which only revealed a little brass-made water pot, beautifully polished. Whenever my thought goes back to such a sight I agree with Pandit Jawahalal Nehru that Indian problems are more economic than political.

Although prepared by previous knowledge I was astounded at the landing wharf of Calcutta to become virtually a captive of beggars with lamentable appeals. And this gloomy experience has again repeated at the Kali Temple where I found difficulty in distinguishing real pilgrims from the begging crowds. Even Chawringi, a fashionable thoroughfare with the best European hotels and museums, was a favourite haunt of beggars and of others who will become beggars at any time. Those homeless people live and die on the public road. If any one kicks their sleeping heads on his way home from a late reception, he is punished by the law, I am told. This is probably an expression of kindness and an act of compensation on the part of the rulers who cannot provide these heads with either a roof or a pillow. Once, on my way to the Japanese Consulate-General near Dalhousie Square, I saw three official trucks overloaded with beggars looking like half-burned firewood or dirty lava. This ghostly spectacle of deformity and disease reminded me of Okyo's scroll of Hell with the damned spirits languishing in their pains. I have no exact knowledge of the number of people belonging to this class, although it must be amazingly large. I cannot help wondering what concern they have with ideas of uplifting their lives, and what benefit they have obtained from modern civilization. You cannot blame them if they are utterly indifferent to their country's problem of independence and freedom, when you think that they are not a creation of one age alone.

We know that two thousand years ago Asoka, a Buddhist emperor, as seen from his monolithic columns and rock edicts in existence today, was certainly an extremely devout and humane man. Admitting his mercy and almsgiving, I do not know what real service he did for elevating the masses of his time. There were many powerful Mohammedan emperors who made their Mughal age distinguished. The grand mien of the Emperor Akbar is traced on the walls of the Agra Fort in granite or marble; the Emperor Shah Jahan built the greatest mausoleum in the world, the Taj Mahal, in memory of his favourite queen, spending some two billion rupees. But we are not told that these emperors popularized the knowledge of letters or that they taught the masses a sense of honour. Road-building in India was left to the British rulers; and it was perfectly accomplished for they had a taste for such a crusade of cement and asphalt. But the low people were again forgotten and their conditions were not one whit improved on those of Buddha's time.

There is, on the other hand, another world, a home of culture and high-thinking, where libraries and fine senate houses cut a figure in Western fashion. As an invited lecturer, I found in this academic world hundreds of brilliant scholars and savants, most of them educated in England, rich in experience of travel. Among the universities I visited, the Hindu University, Benares, comes first to my mind because of the striking contrast of its modernism to the religious fanaticism thriving by the river Ganges as of old. Having inherited all the properties formerly belonging to the Government-General, the University of Delhi delighted me with a huge garden the flowers of which looked so glorious against the purple curtain of the sky. The Osmania University of Hyderabad stands on the billowing breast of a table-land, bare, rouge-coloured, where the Mohammedan professors and students, I thought, could command a splendid situation for evening prayer.

But what surprised me most were the audiences at my lectures, always large and attentive. They caused me to think of the diffusion of English in India and reminded me of the fact that the country has already spent two centuries as a dependency. The English-speaking classes these long years have created there are by no means small, but in comparison with the total population of the country, more than three hundred minions, they are as a drop in the ocean. When I was told that the circulation of such influential papers as the *Statesman,* Calcutta, or the *Times of India*, Bombay, is not larger than fifty thousand, I could not help thinking that the sphere of educated people is sadly confined. Whether or not these educated people, as some Indian critics say, are merely intellectual vagabonds, they have to carry the future of the country on their shoulders. But they should know that nothing can be done without taking thought for the masses, illiterate and dirty, living hardly at subsistence levels.

Even people of my humble class in India lead a materially handsome life with motorcars and servants. They live in houses where, in conformity with climatic needs, the ceilings are high and the windows open on spacious gardens with turf and flowers. Reception after reception was given in my honour, sometimes to my joy and often to my weariness. Being invited by a rich man to dinner, I found that his dining room was paved with marble and that the plates used were all made of silver. I had another surprise when I was told that the salary of a vice-chancellor of a university or a Justice of the Court was not less than forty thousand rupees a year. The contrast between such a salaried upper class and the lowest one composed of naked beggars and coolies makes me think again of the Indian pendulum which, skipping the middle, swings from one extreme to the other.

In interviews with newspapermen, I attributed Japan's rise to her present position as a nation to compulsory education, and incidentally pointed out that the circulation of some Japanese newspapers amounted to two millions. I am by no means an admirer of modern journalism, and sometimes agree with the ancient Chinese sage who said that learning was the father of sorrow; but when even the poorest rag-pickers in Japan are aware through the papers of the movement of the world, I cannot help being thankful for the general education that is diffused throughout our country. Therefore, I said to newspapermen in India: "Give your masses hunger for knowledge! Knowledge points to them the way to improve their lives. Popularization of education is the first and the last. It was painful to learn that ninety persons out of one hundred in India are illiterate. I saw in the third-class railway carriages painted figures of male or female by the side of compartment doors as an indication.

But considering that what the Indian masses immediately need is food rather than books, the possibility of compulsory education is far off. As long as the entanglements of the caste system remain, preventing individual choice in the matter of occupation, education, whatever it may be, cannot be anything but a superfluous burden. What use will be one's knowledge of letters when one's caste demands that one shall become a floor-sweeper?

I visited Waltair, where I lectured overlooking the beautiful Bay of Bengal, Sir Sarpevalli Radakrishnan, the Vice-Chancellor of the University, who presided at my lectures, deplored in the course of private conversation that religious disease in India was chronic. I thought then that he had in his mind the sad penances I observed on the banks of the Ganges and elsewhere. Before I went to India I was told that, because the Mohammedans kill cows, the Hindus, who regard this as a sacred animal, often fight with them to the death on the Mahommedan "Day of Sacrifice." No trouble of a serious nature between the two races came to my knowledge, except the news that with the report that an Indian representative in Africa, a Mohammedan, married a Hindu lady under the promise of conversion, a mass meeting of the Hindus was held in Calcutta as an opposing demonstration.

Mrs. Sarojini Naidu, a Hyderabad poetess and an old friend of mine, invited me to tea one day in Bombay to meet her young Indian friends. All of them, men and women, I found, were handsomely dressed, with the world's culture and taste at their finger-tips. Looking at me with a smile, Madam Naidu asked me: "How many different races are here, do you suppose?" And counting on her fingers, she said: "Just seven!"

I forgot to ask her then how many different languages were used in India.

Contemporary Japan, September 1936

Gazing up to the Southern Hill

I believe that T'ao Ch'ien of China in the fourth century, who "did not bend the hinges of his back for five pecks of rice a day," must have been about my age when, after resigning from the magistracy, he wrote the following lines:

> I raise chrysanthemums by the eastern fence,
> And composed in mind, I gaze up to the Southern
> Hill.

Not flower raising but flower gazing is my present joy. I daresay, however, that I have acquired something of a thoughtful attitude from mountain gazing since my boyhood days; and I am glad that it fits me today as a man sitting on the floor.

I have never been a government official as T'ao Ch'ien once was; so I have not found it necessary to trouble my back reaching for forbidden freedom of speech. I have spent most of my time, praised be God, among books and pictures which I love, and with a few friends who exchange life's joys with the licence of fancy. I am glad that my age makes me search for optimism in nature and art; if the optimism of my own choice has something of epicureanism, that is because I am intuitive rather than intellectual. I confess that, when I talk reminiscently, I am perhaps, like Charles Lamb, too talkative even to the point of impudence.

Again like Lamb, my literary interest is in the gyrations and not in the anticipated conclusion. Although I do not know how I conform with the words of Montaigne, "I write but myself and my essence," I hope that my essays, doubtless not so fluent and intelligible, will reveal the Japanese mind of a thousand years, which defying the law of mutability still exists with some amount of vitality, adapting itself to the new conditions of the modern age.

T'ien Hsia Monthly, December 1936

The Wooden Clogs

Woman is an allegory. She is a formation of tradition and memory, the sum total in figurative expression of old art. She is a vision of beauty, to which our male instinct aspires. The allegory and symbolism melt into one another in her little form; the meaning of the old and new, of the dead and living revive through her. She appears to be a puppet in a lovely scheme of colours, fluttering like a butterfly on magic wings.

What a strange sensation I feel at a puppet play, seeing how suddenly the puppets change from clay to spirit! I have the same feeling when I see the woman of Japan, ghostly as she is, dancing to the accompaniment of music. The ghostly sight of a Japanese woman, free and suggestive, is more significant in the street under the lanterns and by a shop's black drapery with Chinese characters in white. How her shoulders swing in response to the music which her wooden clogs strike on the pavement! What a ghost in happy mood, who roams as the music leads her! I cannot connect her with any purpose in life; I am pleased to think of her as a vagrant ghost who returns from the dusk to fill a moment's joy to please her own fancy. To teach a girl how to wear heavy wooden clogs in her youth is to teach her how to play music with her feet. Who says she is deaf to the music? What our woman plays with her clogs is symbolic—she is simplicity itself, unchangeably young in remembrance of childhood. The music which the woman plays in the street is here too loud there too low. You find variety according to the temperament of the foot-musicians. It is not too much to say that one can distinguish even their beauty (or ugliness) by their manner of playing on the clogs. Is it not true that one seldom mistakes his sweetheart's approach by the sound of her feet?

I cannot forget my first impression (after many years abroad) at the Yokohama station when my ears were suddenly exposed to a volley of music. It was the music which a hurrying mass of women played on the pavement of the platform with their clogs. I was for some time unable to shake off the ghostliness of the monotonous music which the foot-musicians played. The sadness of sound I heard then still haunts my mind even today; its beauty is a kind lone and gray, like that of a caged bell-insect.

How lone and gray is the heart of a Japanese woman! The monotony of her heart is gained from a sacrifice of external effects. It is a spiritual asceticism—the highest prayer. I believe that the beauty of our women's heart has already reached its last evolution. Is not loneliness divine? Is not gray the highest of colours?

T'ien Hsia Monthly, December 1936

The Region beyond the Torii: An Apology

While still a boy ten or eleven years old, I made a miniature hill in my home garden, where I erected a toy torii, an arch standing before a Shinto shrine, and imagined a mysterious region beyond it. This imagination, though vague of course, touched me with awe and delight. Whether it be of stone or wood or bronze, the torii is merely a simple combination of four straight lines; yet as an artistic creation, it has no parallel in the world for symbolical simplicity.

I loved and admired this matchless arch with which even a pyramid or obelisk would not have stood comparison. How glad I was walking in imagination along a mysterious road behind it, and forgetting myself in bliss, holy and strange! There have been in the past many persons like myself, who have looked up to it with curiosity. Korin, for instance, often used this arch in his painting. Hokusai in one of his designs made Mount Fuji peep through it. I do not know where our ancestors first found it or how they happened to build it. Whether it came first from India or from Polynesia, I know that the torii has something which reminds me that it lived with birds ages ago. Look at the curved horizontal line at its top! It makes me think of an undulating billow or a winding hill.

I have said somewhere: "It is a symbol both grand and simple. One has no right to let his earthly ambition enter the arch. Pass through it with prayer or in silence, and reach the place where your temple of art shall be built!" Whether they understood me or not, some of my western friends looked at me aghast and accused me of being afraid of reality. I was often criticised as a conservative through and through, and as a man escaping from the competition which life forces upon us. "Whether or not," they said, "Noguchi prefers western clothes to his native kimono, whether he chooses beefsteak instead of bamboo shoots, we know that his spiritual life is in a temple of old Japan. He is eloquent and even talkative with French cynicism when he protests against the modern type of western invasion in Japan. Is he an old samurai of two swords ready for harakiri?" Not only in the west but even in Japan, in truth, there are not a few people who regard me as a staunch conservative, a propagandist of Orientalism. But am I such an opponent of Occidentalism?

On the other hand there are many, to be sure, who see me as an Occidentalist, a progressionist with a purpose. One in the west who had read in my writings that I "carried Spencer's Education in my pocket as a boy of sixteen, because it was the younger day of new Japan when even we boys thought to educate others before being educated ourselves," was convinced that he had discovered the origin of my existence, and approached me, exclaiming: "Drive away all traditions which are but superstitions! Hallelujah to Japan's new age!" But am I such an Occidentalist as he thinks?

It is true that I often wonder whether I am an Orientalist or Occidentalist, whether I am Japanese or western. This strange question baffles me, and makes me sink into thought. To one who admits my duality, I would reply: "I thank you. You understand me well. If I am Oriental, I am then able perhaps to change art to impassioned vision. And if I am Occidental, I believe that with intellect I can resolve art into a system." I am western when I criticise my Japanese thoughts to discover their international value, while my observation of things western through a Japanese eye makes clear the points that we have in common. Call me a conservative if you like. My conservatism will not be provincial or local because I never deny progress, which is good. Those two things stand in my mind on equal footing. It is said that a shield has two sides. My own soul is one which faces both ways, east and west.

While still young, I went to the west where people hardly knew the difference between Japanese and Polynesians; in the midst of sneers and mockery I assumed the self-appointed office of a Japanese representative in art. I experienced most painful things and was often obliged to stand on the rack. What weapon could I find then to fight with people who were materially richer, scientifically wiser? If there was one, I thought, it should be spiritual. With spiritualism I had to strike the west—it was my plan of operation. My Orientalism was born in the west. It was by no means a caprice like that of people who have much in reserve, because it was the last action by which I cut down a bridge behind me. Although I have written many books in English, the language I use is not that of people born to it; it is the English I picked up at will and arranged as I pleased. What use, I always wonder, is it, to make a human parrot out of myself? My writing in a foreign language is a simple case of missing or hitting the mark. I leave everything to chance. I say to myself amusingly: "But it is the English language that imitates Yone Noguchi. In the matter of language, too, I am an Orientalist." When some English critic commented that what I wrote passed by his ears, without permeating his head, he was quite right. And again when he said, "Of course it may be that I think differently from him," he was right too.

But my Orientalism, whatever it be, shakes me awfully when I find myself in circumstances where I should know the strong points of the west, and makes me think that two peoples, the Oriental and the Occidental, on one pair of shoulders are too painful to carry about. If I were only a Japanese, or only a westerner, I think I would be better off.

Now to return to the beginning, there is beyond the torii a holy region, a land of twilight, where neither the west nor the east is distinct. At such a place where time and space prevail under one blessing, it is foolish to discuss the Oriental or the Occidental. But if I carry on my shoulders two races at the present moment, I should be happy to carry them. It is certainly better to have two than one.

T'ien Hsia Monthly, December 1936

The One-Hundredth

"Once determined, I could easily make a criminal of myself," I say. "But that determination is the question. Can I, after all, give myself to crime?" Supposing that I stop and think just before the final decision to do some vicious thing. I pity my own spiritless self and even study where timidity builds a nest in my mind. But I am far from believing that I am pure and clean. Like many others, I hate and loathe to be ruled and limited by fact, for, like a chained dog, my soul works unconsciously to find relief, although she is uncertain about her real nature. I believe that ninety-nine men out of one hundred are neither gods nor devils. I have lived till today charmed by the dream that I could accomplish something great. To save misapprehension, I should say that I have thought that some special chance would be given me some day, when I could express, distinctly and truly, my own nature in writing as well as in action. Not even once in my life have I knowingly acted a falsehood which injured my honour. But feeling that I have somehow been unable to bring out the best in me, I cannot help thinking how much good the ninety-nine mediocrities will do, if I miss being the one-hundredth. If I did not tell the final truth, I should be punished for my negation. The simple fact that I did not play with falsehood would not be worth a brass farthing.

I have used a great deal of ink in the past on my poems and prose; it seems that my work was merely a record of comings and goings on the same mental road. My literary ink suddenly dried up when I had managed to approach the one-hundredth, the most important point of all. There is evidence that I even shrank from reaching that point. Am I a sluggish idler who potters away his time? We have a word "Ocha-wo-Nigosu," meaning "To wriggle out of the matter." In literature as well as in life, nine hundred and ninety-nine men out of one thousand are only clever enough to make a good face publicly. And we are seldom given a chance for the expression of final truth, even when we are ready for it.

The late Admiral Togo, a great sailor who defeated the Baltic fleet of Russia during the Russo-Japanese war, exclaimed to his forlorn and hopeless staff at the moment of their departure: "The rise or fall of our Empire depends on this one battle!" The chance for such a great cry, however, falls on a fighter of any country only once in a thousand years. Only one who faced life with bridges burned behind him would be able to act like General Nogi who killed himself to escort the soul of the departed emperor. I will mention Basho among the literary men of Japan as one who expressed the "one-hundredth." At his dying hour, it is said, Basho was asked by his disciples to give them his farewell poem. Basho replied to them: "Anything of mine will do well for that purpose, because I wrote each poem under the impression that it was a farewell word." Rather to this attitude toward poetry than to his actual poems, I bend my head in reverence. It is never too much to say that he dealt with poetry like a man fighting with a real sword: he was a stag at bay in literature.

But there are many instances when men clever and rich in natural endowment stopped at the ninety-ninth and could not burn their boats for the final expression of the one-hundredth. I know that many people of the past renounced the world for monkhood and withdrew themselves into a valley or mountain for prayer. When poets of the past jealously guarded their single blessedness and rendered themselves free of life's fetters, they were making ready, like bird-catchers under the bushes, for a sight of the most important chance for the final outcry. If a modern poet dreams of living in a castle and at the same time writing a worthy poem, he will find it as impossible and foolish as to find a fish among the branches of a tree.

When my thoughts are related to those of the race type, I feel greatly relieved and even light-hearted, because of a sense of mutual responsibility which often means irresponsibility. But when, aloof from those of my own race, my thoughts belong to me alone, I cannot help feeling heavy and even depressed by my sense of responsibility for them. But that heaviness of feeling, if I have it, is nothing but the highest joy a man can have in solitude where there is no one to talk with except his own shadow on the wall. I know that at the climax when parted from actuality, freedom would become the very source of the joy which mingles with a sense of sadness, and again would become the very source from which real poetry springs.

No one can develop anything, small or large, without the agency of habit; one's habit is the "invitation water" that makes the well-pump effective. Once I visited a cathedral in France where there was nothing to disturb the unworldly old atmosphere which softly tightened my pagan mind with mystery; if there was anything to break the silence that flooded the place, It was my slow footsteps to which the pavement echoed, and which led me to an enclosed recess where the confessional was. "What confession do I have," I wondered, for confessing was not in the habit of my Oriental life. "But I might make up something at first," I thought next, "and if I keep on repeating it, I am sure that my real confession will then come out naturally."

We should make a habit of writing, and of course of living; even a falsehood will be excused when it becomes an "invitation water" to the good habit that follows after. Credit should be given for expression which reaches ninety-nine, provided it comes through good habit. But we should destroy it and forget it for the most important one-hundredth chance that may appear by accident.

T'ien Hsia Monthly, December 1936

The Sense of Amazement

The world of an art collector is strange, almost mysterious. He gropes for the Accidental which is vulgarly called a find; with minute attention, inscrutable to others, he is seen prying about with a wandering eye which, if you will excuse a disrespectful comparison, makes me think of that of a pickpocket. His is not the ordinary eye of ordinary people, because, being keen in the sense of amazement, it has something of the madman or the witch; we call it the mind's eye. The capacity for wonder is one touchstone by which the qualifications of a collector are measured. I mean that the strength of your sensibility must be tested.

From another angle, the collector must be eager almost to the point of obstinacy like a hero in love; and with the witchery of passion, he must lure out his object from its hiding place and make it approach him and finally fall into his pit. We say that all is fair in love. Like men in love, the collector is also blind. An art dealer once said this to me:

"Why, he is impossible; I do not know what to do with him when he comes to my shop. His dogged persistence does not budge even an inch till he possesses the thing he came for. Overcome by his zeal, I always surrender my fort to him unwittingly. I have no time to think of the price when he marches against me with such enthusiasm. I cannot help thinking: 'All right! Take it away as quickly as possible! I will give it to you to be rid of you.' Then I experience the loneliness that follows the consciousness of my losing the thing for an unusually low price, and I hate him, despise him, even denounce him as an annoying bore or nuisance. But as I think a moment later that the safety of the arts depends solely on such people as him, he becomes worthy and even acquires a halo. Art dealing is to me a strange business, an extraterritoriality in the commercial world, where I alternately curse and admire my customers—then myself too."

I myself know two or three collectors of the type my friend the dealer talked of, and with respect I open wide my door in welcome to them, and receive them as my friends into my humble sanctum where I spin my spider-web of poetry. There is no happier or more satisfactory time, I declare, than when I listen to their stories of the anxiety and care they have undergone for their collections; I thank them for their assurance that their world of dust-smelling hanging-rolls or armless idols is as true and real as mine. Ours are the worlds of excitement which are at their highest when the excitement subsides, and selected people who are capable of amazement and rapt appreciation of true and beautiful things congregate here together with only one song.

Once one of those collectors told me the following story in a mood of reminiscence:

"It was late one night some fifteen years ago that my tram-car ran slowly up the slope toward the Denzu-in Temple from Hongo; my story, however, has nothing to do with the temple. I think I should have told you at the beginning that I felt something in my mind that night, which you might call preperception. Of course it was not clear what it was. But I was tickled somehow by the feeling that I would come across some good painting, and then I felt uneasy accordingly. When my tram-car passed by the temple, I was drowsily toying with the premonition of making some good find. I looked mechanically through the car-window at the shops shifting like magic lantern slides, when I caught a glimpse of a picture of a beautiful woman, who beckoned to me from a curio-shop. I got off the car when it stopped, and walked back to the shop, wondering if my preperception was not for that woman. A few minutes later I stood gazing at the picture. It was evident that the shop-owner thought it a forgery, because the price he wanted for it was ridiculously low. But my instinct proclaimed its genuineness. I bought it and took it home humming a song of victory, hoisting a joyous flag. Praised be God, a genuine Shunsho for a petty ten yen note! I pinched myself to be sure I was not dreaming.

"When I reached home, I unrolled the hanging in which the beautiful woman drawn by Shunsho, a master artist of the print world of Japan, was choking with dust. I at once rescued her from this unpleasant condition, for I carefully dusted the picture which I hung a moment later in a dimly lighted alcove. The woman was young, dressed in black Sukiya, a thin silken stuff, after the fashion of the Kansei period, its sombreness brightened by a wide sash of vermilion crepe spotted with white; and from underneath the dress the pleasantly swelling contours of her body showed with an excusable touch of sensuality. She carried a large round fan in her hand, with which she meant to catch fireflies, the will-o-the-wisps of a Japanese summer night; in the background late iris flowers were still blooming.

"Excuse me for my detailed description of the work, for it soon became one of the treasures in my collection which is by no means great. I do not think that the world of art alone is mysterious—of course not! But when I think that many valuable things the past masters created with effort and patience are still buried and forgotten under spider-webs or dust, I cannot help feeling that the office of collectors becomes important, even dignified with a pride like that of a scientist or discoverer. How thankful I was that night, you can imagine, for the preperception that prophesied truly!"

I agreed with him and thanked him because incidentally he expressed and endorsed my opinions on the matter of poetry. When Basho of the seventeenth century noticed a lone violet by the mountain-side, and when Wordsworth sang of the small celandine, daisy and daffodil—those botanical fairies seldom praised by poets before his time—both of them were psychologically on the same plane as my collector friend when he found Shunsho's woman. Blessed be the men who can respond promptly to beautiful things when they see them! But this sense of amazement is a by-product of love. Therefore love is the main issue.

Without love nothing worthy can be done in the world. Before you write poetry you must understand what love is. Without love a painter cannot draw even one blade of grass, and a collector cannot see the real worth of Shunsho or any other artist when it appears before his face. Without love you cannot knead bread or build a fire.

T'ien Hsia Monthly, December 1936

Calligraphy and Painting

I called the other day on an artist friend who has forsaken western for Japanese painting and who excels in still life, making vegetables his speciality. I found him busy studying calligraphy. He said to me:

"There is nothing more familiar and more welcome to us than vegetables, because, besides providing wholesome nourishment, they give us a modest and peaceful smell reminding us of the soil. Flowers are less familiar to us, I should say, for unless we use more pigments to represent their form exactly, they may remain unrecognized. Although we try to patronise birds and even call them beloved, the fact is that we know very little about them, and when a painter approaches them, they reject his intimacy by flying away and one has no chance for close observation. Of course there are many reference books left by artists of former times, but these do not enable us to excel them in the subject. Besides, we are not strong enough to be independent of the old masters. So I say that we should leave birds alone. But vegetables—a cabbage, an onion, a potato and a carrot—are different, because we can touch and fondle them, play with them and kiss them if we want. The best of all is that, since we know them familiarly, people do not expect the painter to draw them so minutely, and even without colouring, they know at once what they are. Just a few lines, provided they are well drawn, are enough for a radish or turnip. My study of calligraphy is meant to make those few lines graceful. As far as I am concerned, painting and calligraphy stand on an equal basis. Therefore I am glad to spend the whole morning of such a lovely day as this on one ideographic character."

I thanked my friend because his remark agreed with what I have in mind and he inspired me to consider the question more fully. Ideographs—Chinese characters—as the name indicates have their origin in pictures drawn from the imagination of the first inventor; being a mixture of picture and of what belongs to the character alone, they are symbols in a state of flux, general rather than specific. And conversely we can say that, when the picture dissolves, we see its most elementary form in the ideograph. The lines, straight or curving, which constitute Chinese characters, relate closely to pictures, for, although they do not always exist in the actual things pictured the lines have their beginning where the picture begins, and their ending where it finishes. I mean that the lines sometimes express the meaning or the development of a picture, and sometimes that of the completion of it. But it is far more interesting and true to see them at the intersection of these two expressions than to see them as either separately, because the lines should constitute a symbol of the final form of life and nature where the beginning and the ending, the positive and the negative, congregate and hug each other. And such a blending as this can be realised, not in a developed form of expression but in an embryo form where individuality is not concrete. It is natural that, whether in the form of beginning or of ending some Oriental artists belonging to the vegetables, a few lines which correspond with those of a Chinese character are enough for his radish or turnip.

Wu Tao-tsu of the T'ang dynasty is cited as a successful blender of painting and calligraphy; and it is said that he often complained of the difficulty of excelling in the latter, because one's mental greatness, lofty and unaffected by sentiment, alone enables one to keep its original integrity lighted by the faint glamour of pictorial suggestion. When Chao Sung-hsüeh of a later date, one of the propagandists of this unification, left a dictum, "A stone must be painted in the fei-pai style, a tree in the liu-chuan style and a bamboo in the pa-fa style," according to the "eight radical principles of calligraphy," he had fallen into a mannerism where art was hampered by theory. But I Yün-lin, a well-known contemporary of Chao Sung-hsüeh, declared: "What I call a painting is nothing more than a work of rapid handling, regardless of transcription from nature. I am satisfied to express myself in painting." He jealously guarded the beauty of a twilight land where painting and calligraphy abide as one. But he forgot to speak of his satisfaction in calligraphy.

Following those Chinese artists or diverging from them, we find in Japan a side issue, a somewhat different pictorial branch and leaf, where many artists put a few parallel lines for a river and a few dots for a group of birds. I do not want however to dwell on the history of calligraphic art, because it suffices to say that it was originated by those who in a gentlemanly and leisurely pursuit related themselves through calligraphy to pictures in shadowy embryo. Hence the name of the Literati School.

"Whether or not you belong to the Literati School," I exclaimed to the artist of onions and carrots, "you withdraw into archaism where your pictorial line is an enigma. Take me for a student, my dear fellow, for I am growing quite old and calligraphy becomes attractive. Will you laugh at me then if I pretend to be interested in it from the standpoint of a painter?"

T'ien Hsia Monthly, December 1936

Debussy in Japan

A few years ago I acted as artistic guide to a famous musician of the West at Horyuji in Nara, one of the most ancient Buddhist temples of the early seventh century; the visitor's enthusiasm made him declare that he was born in Europe by mistake. I was glad that, being with this enthusiast, westernized Japan dressed in American fashion meekly retired from our presence when we visited Horyuji Temple where religious integrity was undisturbed and the red autumnal foliage was beautiful. Right or wrong, we are human beings who, without apology, go to extremities and openly embrace them according to the whims of our mental pendulums; as for me I become at once ultra-Japanese when my Occidentalism leaves me alone. When I step into the temple ground, I try to read from ideographs floating in air the history of a thousand years ago when Shotoku Taishi, son of the Emperor Yomei and the founder of the temple, loomed up in the image of Buddha wearing a monk's scarf.

Perhaps my Western friend understood my mental condition at that moment and was afraid to break its serenity, for he walked with stealthy steps and bowed head on the stones leading towards the five-storied pagoda, where the tiny sun-plants smiled bashfully up to the sky. The sky was purple. The air smelled sweet. We could not help then giving thanks to this autumnal joy that lifted us into air like the dragonflies, aeroplanes with dark-red tails, which we saw about the lowest roof of the pagoda. At the four corners of the roof shining with sea-green moss, there hung four little bells of the same green. We looked up at them when they rang their brief simple note, played by a passing breeze. My musician-friend turned to me and exclaimed with a smile, "Why, that's Debussy!"

Now let me take you next into the inmost heart of the mountainous province of Kaga for another scene, where, some years ago, I went searching after the beauty of plum blossoms that, as recorded by Setsudo Saito, a well-known scholar of the Chinese classics, infold the valley stream from both sides with feathery hangings of white. The scene is again a Buddhist temple which, unlike the preceding one famous in history, only receives an occasional visitor when the flowers bloom. The name of the temple is Shinfuku, meaning "Real Wealth." Since one's real wealth lies in mental peace, undisturbed by modern machinery, jazz bands or automobiles, this name is fully justified because the temple, a trifling thing really, is snug with all the blessings of mountain trees and, of course, of the plum trees which, responding to the call of fate, throw down their snow-petals to decorate the ground.

Although Setsudo advises a visit to the temple at night when the moon writes a flower-poem and paints the ground with the intermingled shadows of the plum trees, my calling at the place in the afternoon when time had forgotten to move, was not without delight, because this little village temple appeared to be a symbol of mental abandonment in the kingdom of emptiness. My tired soul and my tired body, for I had travelled three hundred miles from home, grew at once composed in the soothing atmosphere of antique origin as if I had taken a narcotic. I approached the temple with its roof thatched in mushroom fashion; and I opened one of its front sliding-doors, expecting the reply of the old temple-master from within. No voice responded to me at all. I waited attentively for another two minutes. Still no reply came. Then I recalled Li Po of the middle of the eighth century in China, who, climbing up the mountain to find his priest friend away, had written on the temple door a poem with the following lines:

Sweet scented clouds are wafted along the moun-
tain-side,
And a rain of flowers falls from the sky.
Here I may taste the bliss of solitude
And listen to the plaint of blue monkeys!

Instead of Li Po's "blue monkeys," I found here a cock and a few hens, all of them black-coated in Hamlet fashion, walking with halting steps on the ground that expanded between the gate tower and the temple; on this cleanly swept ground many plum petals had fallen, endorsing Li Po's poem. I stood aside and gazed at the feathery Hamlets, silent because they were wise, who turned on me sideward glances, as if whispering: "Beware, this is a secret place of isolation from the world! Swear, swear that you will never tell others about our joy!" At this moment I heard from a shed behind the temple the sound of rice being hulled in a stone mortar, the sound breaking the tranquillity of the place,—tong, tong, tong, tong! Instantly I wondered: "What would my Western musician-friend say if he were here? Would he find Debussy in that sound? Who then, if not Debussy?"

An autumnal shower makes me think of my friend's famous play, Sakura Shigure, because its success depends solely on the poetical atmosphere the shower inspires. As a playwright he is cunning enough to withhold the appearance of the shower till the fourth act when people expect something to turn up. I have no mind to dwell on the details of the play; let it suffice to say that, overtaken by the shower, Shoyu, famous tea-man and father of Saburobei whom he had disowned because of his liaison with Yoshino the courtesan, accidentally took shelter at a wretched cottage where the autumnal shower sang a melody on silvery strings in Debussy fashion. This cottage was his son's love-refuge of which Shoyu had no knowledge at all. Yoshino whom he had despised without seeing, now before him but not identified, entertained him with a cup of tea. Before he thanked her for her consideration in making his stop delightful, Shoyu was surprised to discover an ideal tea-devotee in Yoshino when he saw how gracefully she made the tea. I will leave to the readers' imagination how the story advances, because my present interest is in the autumnal shower playing on the roof in accompaniment to the boiling tea-kettle. Who will doubt that these two natural musicians, the shower and the tea-kettle, would please an artist of Debussy's temperament?

Once some years ago when I visited Kyoto in autumn to see the beauty of the maple leaves, and wandered about the riverside of Arashiyama, I was obliged to take temporary shelter from a sudden shower at a nondescript farm-house, rich only in the bamboo forest that furnished an impressive background. I was cordially received by a woman, plainly dressed but young and beautiful, who, according to the fashion of the place, offered me a ceremonial cup of tea. She had lovely little fingers that could never have belonged to one of the labouring class. I fancied that she was another Yoshino escaped from a sensual quarter of wine and song. In the front yard the chrysanthemums were blooming, their rouged lips beautifully moistened by the shower, soft and kind. The afternoon sunlight almost gold in colour, began suddenly to flame up the sparsely-set silver bars of rain that kept falling slantwise. The eaves-drops repeated their monotonous song in the fashion of a Buddhist prayer making me wish for the presence of my Western musician-friend who had discovered Debussy on the lips of temple bells.

T'ien Hsia Monthly, February 1937

Floral Beauty

Early in the morning I left the mountain tavern, "Riding-on-Stork Pavilion," an out-of-the-way place, where I had spent the night doubting the beauty of the plum blossoms of this place for which I had taken the trouble to come three hundred miles. I was glad, however, that my departure took place when the brilliant morning sun was rising to open all the sliding-doors of the valley, mysterious and dark, and when rehabilitating their fame, the plum blossoms smiled to me in pearly white. The morning air was fresh and pungent. My descending steps were light along a narrow path through dwarfish tea-trees, botanical monks in meditation whose black robes, now with the dew brightened by sunlight, were changed to ultramarine fit for the apparel of a Pope. Raising my face to the mountain over the river, I noticed that the trees, cedars and pines, had scarcely cast off their night-gowns of fog and cloud, but exchanged delightfully a word of morning greeting to one another. Then breaking the quiet atmosphere of solitude, my agile footsteps followed down by the river where a thousand plum trees used its limpid clear water for their toilet mirror. I could not help exclaiming: "How beautiful, how beautiful they are!"

After half an hour when I was almost at the point of leaving the whole valley to another man's possession, I turned back to look at the "Riding-on-Stork Pavilion," a black speck which God the painter had dropped on the mountain's breast. I thought, forgetting the sneers I had entertained before, that, since the tavern looked like the aerial refuge of a saintly person who went about on a stork's back, its name was fully justified; and I even wished that I could return to test whether or not I could fit into that unworldly place. Though not distinct, there were a few fragmentary banners of cloud and torn ribbons of fog that protected the house with their blessing, turning it into a hermit's home like that of an old picture. My visit to this flower valley in Iga province was well worth the trouble of those three hundred miles, I thought, though I had not realized it before; and then an old desire to become a painter revived in me. "Riding-on-Stork Pavilion from the Distance" would have made a good subject.

If I were a good painter of the decorative school, I would not fail to draw a scene upon a huge canvas like an eight-leaf screen, where golden blossoms of the rape-seed are in their glory, covering the sea-flat ground with the sun and moon on the right and left, low in the sky and misty as in the afternoon. In London many years ago, when I stood on Westminster Bridge, I was greeted by the sun and moon at the same time through an early spring fog; and since that time I have wondered why they cannot appear in Japan simultaneously to praise the beautiful world, when the rape-seeds paint the ground in gold. My reminiscence of boyhood days as far as flowers are concerned, begins with the rape-seeds that are richest in my native town, the sea-wide field of which is intersected diagonally by one large dyke where the dragon-shaped pine trees read prayers. If I remember rightly the wind, particularly in spring, used to blow them more gently and more softly than today. How often I turned my steps towards this dyke, satiating my mind with a juvenile dream of Lancelot who, if he were there, would be mounting on a white charger with gemmed bridle and sounding a golden bugle to the high sky. I even made a wooden shield with the picture of a lady in the centre, ready for the time when I should become a mediaeval knight. Although this Western symbol of chivalry and youth ceased to exist long ago, the beautiful field of rape-seed in gold still remains in my mind, where, like square-poem papers blown by the wind, the butterflies fly up and down.

Again I wished I were a painter, if possible in the fashion of Sotatsu who delightfully compressed nature's physical beauty into a decorative synthesis when a few years ago I saw a scene where the burning fire of azaleas in red congregating in a large thicket at one side brightened the darkness of a garden. What a beautiful contrast of colours, red and black, there was in the scene! Praising his sense of beauty, I thought the master of the garden was fortunate when he told me that on account of the azaleas the wild encroachment of night had been delayed for at least an hour. Then he added that, if he lighted the stone lanterns in his garden that precious one hour would be prolonged to two hours. I was glad that this flower lover was like an ancient Chinese who, grudging every minute of the passing spring, carried his lantern to light up the flowers till midnight. I thought that he was qualified to be a "Man mad with Flower-gazing." If I were a painter who specializes in flowers, I thought afterwards that it would not be bad at all to be called an "Old Man mad in Painting a Floral Lady."

I have a few things in my home garden, of which I can be proud; for instance, the umbrella-pine with all its symmetry of branches, and the large mignonette with an odour that makes me recall a thousand and one things; but above the rest, I deem precious and dear the wistaria tree which, though today it is big and grand enough to adorn any Daimyo's garden, was only a trifle given to me as a sort of premium when I planted it there twenty years ago. Since this wistaria grows like an awning beside a corridor forty feet long, I can admire its blossoms, even while lying down on the dingy floor of my little study, or touch and fondle their tassels when I pass by. According to the common saying, my wistaria too may love wine to make its blossoms longer, but I am sorry that I cannot satisfy its desire for I am not in the same class as the old Chinese poet who conquered the universe with a jugful of wine. Still loyal to me, my friend offers me blossoms two feet long every spring.

Apart from being a moralist who finds virtue in any old

thing, I am not anxious to discover a feminine ideal in wistaria; I do not care to make it a floral emblem of gentleness or obedience, the keynote of a Japanese woman's beauty, because of its gentle falling down. But if I were a painter cunning in figure-drawing, I would surely draw a beautiful young woman carrying a few trailing sprays of this purple flower, and make her dance in sorrow as she bids farewell to spring. It is true that, when this spirit of the last flower of spring departs, another dancer—the morning-glory—will be quite ready to appear on the scene.

In an essay on the morning-glory I said: "The relationship of the flower to the breath and odour of the summer dawn is exactly the same as my relation to it; I am glad to read myself through its presence my own strength of impulse towards nature and song. What a stretch of vines, what force hardly conceivable as belonging to the vegetable kind and what a more than human sensitiveness. It is no wonder that one can read every change of the hour and even minute of the day in this flower's look and attitude." I am afraid such language might lead one to mistake me for a professional horticulturist who is delighted to create in the morning-glory the floral wonder of a dragon's moustache or a hanging bell. Not at all! I am merely a common person who satisfies himself with a few pots bought from a flower-vender who passes by in the streets. "Here are your pots, sir,"—the same old florist would say to me whom I have known for many years and who comes unfailingly every year and exclaims: "See how beautiful they are this year! I give them plenty of fertilizer. Besides the weather has been good and kind. Please, sir, feed them with strong sunlight! And don't forget to water them plentifully when the noon whistle blows! Good-bye, sir, till next summer!"

My old wife is glad to find a new job, befitting her age, watering the morning-glories; since she is nothing if not punctual, she is to be seen with a little toy-like sprinkler in the garden where the pots, twenty of them, are placed in order, when the watering hour comes. She even asks me to take them up to the roof of the house when the sun becomes dark and veiled. I cannot help entertaining a little fear that she may rush at any minute into the dangerous condition of a morning-glory maniac or horticulturist. As for me, I remain a common person who owes the flower many thanks for making him an early riser.

"A face praising the summer dawn,—a face spilling tears for joy too great,—a face with lips apart, charmed by the sun,—a face wild yet tender,—a face only too happy to die when all its adorations are told."

T'ien Hsia Monthly, February 1937

The Bamboo Thicket

It was a Chinese literary fancy not to see a bamboo as a bamboo only, when, as one of the "four gentlemen," bamboo, orchid, plum, and chrysanthemum, it was raised to a superior rank in the botanical world. The Chinese discovered in the bamboo a "distinguished virtue that belongs to the cool breeze"; discovering a human bond with it, they yielded themselves, consciously or not, to a sense of pantheism.

There have been in the past many Chinese artists to whom the bamboo became a favourite subject and through which they laboured for the improvement of artistic personality. It was natural that as Confucian believers they should go further and take the bamboo even for an object lesson in morality, making of their art an ethical conception. Whether you take it for merit or for demerit depends on your mental barometer; at all events such an attitude explains in a great measure the psychology of the Chinese, the wisest and oldest nation in the world.

Although there are many in Japan who will swallow a Chinese dose, whether good or bad, my own concern with things in nature is purely artistic, influenced by neither virtue nor morality, because, aside from the bamboo itself, for instance, I take delight in its association with other things. Since natural phenomena, however various, are of identical quality,—all dancers moved by one song, and have no antipathy among themselves, it seems that if selection is allowed to the bamboo, it should be happy in the company of snow and sparrows in winter, and of moonlight and the cuckoo in summer. Among my favourite Hokku poems on the bamboo is the following:

A cuckoo cries:
Through the bamboo thicket comes
The moonlight a-straying.

The summer night, already deep, is supposed to be smoking in purple under the moonlight when like a rocket, one sharp note of the cuckoo falls to the ground where the bamboos are thickest. Blessed by the straying moonlight, the celestial guest of night, the thicket responds in joyous thrill to the nocturnal call of the bird. Oh, what a beautiful and quiet scene it is!

Because of the bamboo thicket that richly flourishes there, I never fail to call at Arashiyama when I am in Kyoto. Not only at Arashiyama but in other places near the old capital, I often find a bamboo thicket that surprises me delightfully by its size. If I had lived in the third century in China and had been one of the "Seven Sages of the Bamboo Grove," I would have established my literary club here and fed the bamboo roots with the wine that spilled from my cup. I have read somewhere that they love wine. Like Buson, poet and painter of the eighteenth century, who praised the beauty of young bamboo shoots under the sunset glow of spring, I used to take my evening walk towards a bamboo thicket which I discovered at some distance from my home at Higashi Nakano, although it has been long since destroyed; with delight touched by sorrow, I often observed there that, like the long rich hair of Rossetti's Damozel falling from the rampart of Heaven, the shadow of evening came creeping to change the youthfulness of the leaves to a maturity of grey. Finding no one there, I was sometimes frightened when the bamboo replied to the wind passing by toward its own nightly rest. I recall a large thicket of these "botanical gentlemen" which I saw many years ago in the suburbs of Singapore where my fancy took me in the faint hope of finding an elephant or giraffe; although it was late in October, the hot tropical sunlight overflowed on the leaves and every moment changed their dark gloss. What exuberance was in their colour and form! Seeing before me such a regiment of bamboos endorsing Su Tung-po's words, "leaving the earth as high as the sky," I could not help wondering at the grandeur of God's scheme which I had never seen before in my life. In contrast to nature at home, self-composed and quiet, though it is not so hardened as to reveal the "virtue or morality" which the Chinese discovered in bamboo, here at Singapore all trees, all flowers and all grasses, like human beings, are half-naked or wholly naked, putting aside petty proprieties and manners for a barbarous exposition of passion. I looked about with a sense of amazement at this boundless life which God has instilled into all trees, and I wondered what association with other phenomena I should give to the bamboos. The tropical night was gorgeous and lovely, and the moonlight suited the picture, although I was restless and uncomfortable in my search for solitude. But would the cuckoo break the summer night? Could I expect it to throw a single rocket of sound into this burning place, I wondered? I will ask an ornithologist at the first chance whether or not the cuckoo is a tropical bird.

I sometimes venture to think that there was originally only one long hot season throughout the year in Japan, till the cold wind and snow encroached upon it from the Arctic Circle and finally adjusted the climate into four seasons. Of course that was a billion years ago when no Japanese lived in the islands. Since many of our ancestors came from the South Seas where people are all sailors and their houses are simple in the extreme, and since we see clay and wattles in Japan even today, it is quite natural that in the hot summer time our blood should unconsciously awake to an ancient memory and cry in home-sickness.

Who can doubt that the singing hearts of the cicadas are burning in summer for the South Seas where mangosteens ripen and hibiscus blooms? Again who knows if the soul of my beloved bamboo is not weeping with the intensity of nostalgia.

T'ien Hsia Monthly, February 1937

The Future of Democracy

The present international situation reminds me of the time, twenty-five years ago, when we were asked to choose between an energy-civilization, based on power, and a morality-civilization based on cosmic law of harmony. A truly great society cannot be one that turns back upon itself and tears itself to pieces. For many years, we Japanese have been reading English books describing a democratic civilization developed step by step on liberal, even ethical, principles. The outstanding quality of such a civilization must be its power to survive, regulated by its own sense of honor, conscious of its responsibility for humanity. A nation that seeks harmonious development, even under difficult circumstances, will not become a victim of wild dreams or self-indulgence. Japan will be heavily indebted to such a democratic civilization as that of America if it manages to avoid ruthless ambition and materialism, and to remain safely on the middle path between fascism and communism. It is certainly a mistake to think that Japan is now embarked on a fascist course.

The world at present is badly confused; following a safe path is a matter of momentous importance. Material interests hamper the effort to maintain mental equilibrium. Nevertheless, it can be done. One cannot comment on the comparative merits of authoritarian government and democracy without at the same time pointing out that each country has its own special problems and must find its own way in the light of history. If the national spirit remains secure, I see no reason why, for the individual, security and freedom should be incompatible. Look forward with hope, believe in the future.

The New Republic, 12 May 1937

Notes

1 *Time* 50 (28 July 1947): 84.
2 Sherard Vines, "The English Poetry of Yone Noguchi," *India and the World* 3:12 (Dec. 1934), 354.
3 Marianne Moore, *The Selected Letters of Marianne Moore*, ed. Bonnie Costello (New York: Knopf, 1997), 313.
4 Francis Bickley, "Yone Noguchi's Essays," *Bookman* (London) 45 (Feb. 1914): 275.
5 [Arthur Waley], "Japanese Essays and Poems," *TLS*, 6 Apr. 1922, 227.
6 Padraic Colum, "Japanese Artistry," *Freeman* 5 (22 Mar. 1922): 43-44.
7 Noguchi to *The Dial*, 28 Nov. 1928, Scofield Thayer Papers, Beinecke Library.
8 See Shuang Shen, "*T'ien Hsia:* Cosmopolitanism in Crisis," *Cosmopolitan Publics: Anglophone Print Culture in Semi-Colonial Shanghai* (New Brunswick: Rutgers University Press, 2009), 59-93.
9 The variant essays omitted here are "The No or Mask Play of Japan," *China Journal* 10:3 (March 1929): 113-116 and "Three Scenes from Japanese No Plays," in *Life and Letters To-day* 13:2 (Dec. 1935): 32-40, which are incorporated in "The Mask Play of Japan"; and "All the Arts Are One," a combined and reedited version of "Japanese Art" and "Japanese Poetry" published in *Asia* 37 (Feb. 1937): 121-26.

Noguchi Project Editions
Series Editor: Edward Marx

This series was created to offer carefully edited standard editions of the major writings and critical heritage of Yone Noguchi and his circle.

The text follows that of the original publications except where typographical and transcription errors and irregularities of punctuation have been corrected.

Cover illustration
Ogata Korin, *Bamboo and Plum Tree*, early eighteenth century, Tokyo National Museum.

Frontispiece:
Yone Noguchi in the waiting room at the Asahi Shimbun Company lecture hall, Sukiyabashi, Tokyo, Fall 1926, from Toyama Usaburo, *Shijin Yone Noguchi Kenkyu*, volume 2.

www.ingramcontent.com/pod-product-compliance
Lightning Source LLC
LaVergne TN
LVHW050649100826
845148LV00011B/2050

* 9 7 8 0 6 1 5 7 6 5 4 3 3 *